SCIENTISTS AND TECHNOLOGISTS

By the Same Author

Eminent Indians: Freedom Fighters
Eminent Indians: Musicians
Eminent Indians: Economists and Industrialists
Eminent Indians: Litterateurs
Eminent Indians: Film Personalities
Eminent Indians: Dancers
Eminent Indians: Saints and Sages
Eminent Indians: Legal Luminaries
Eminent Indians: Ten Great Artists
Eminent Indians: Political Thinkers and Administrators

Eminent Indians

SCIENTISTS AND TECHNOLOGISTS

M.L. Ahuja

Rupa & Co

My parents
who, though no more, have been
the source of inspiration to me.

Contents

Preface

Science and technology in India have made great strides since the Vedic times. Ancient Indian thinkers and philosophers like Panini, Patanjali, Aryabhatta, Sushruta, among others, made pioneering contributions in different areas of man's thought and culture, both spiritual and material. During the last two centuries, India's potentiality for learning has blossomed further under the impact of Western critical scholarship in sophisticated scientific knowledge. Today Indians have made their mark as leading scientists and technical experts the world over.

Ancient India's contribution to the medical sciences was of a high order. Available data suggest a fairly advanced knowledge of surgery during the Harappan civilisation. Information culled from the *Atharvaveda* betrays belief in demons of disease and prescription of spells as cure. But the *Charaka Samhita* suggests a great improvement in the knowledge of medical science as also Nagarjuna's redaction of the *Sushruta Samhita*, both of which deal with eight different branches of medical science. While the *Charaka Samhita* contains, *inter alia*, an exhaustive discussion on therapeutic medicine, the major subject of the *Sushruta Samhita* is surgery. Both the treatises also discuss the methods of attaining rejuvenation, thereby indicating knowledge of alchemy. Progress in medical science during the Gupta Age is evident from the work done on garlic (*lasuna*) and others that cure several diseases.

Indian philosophers, pioneered by Patanjali, also contributed to the medical sciences. The Yoga system of philosophy, with its mental and physical discipline, ensures the functioning of the human body in a state of perfect health and flexibility. This philosophy advocates an integrated system of mental concentration, breath control, sense control and a refined physical culture, involving voluntary and involuntary muscles, through which many pathological conditions can be cured. Indian Ayurveda, or 'Science of Life', is not restricted to mere medical knowledge. It includes subjects like climatology, philosophy, etc., which do not come within the scope of formal medical science. The Ayurveda, which considers medical treatment as a process of restoration of lost equilibrium of *doshas* (morbidity of the body caused by imbalance in *vayu*, *pitta* and *kapha*) and *dhatus* (body constituents), has certain distinguishing features marking it as a unique type of medical system.

The *Ashtanga-samgraha* and *Ashtanga-hridaya-samhita* by Vagbhata are two great works in medical science. The *Rugvinischaya* (or *Madhava-nidana*) by Madhava tries to bring to perfection the branch of pathology. The *Dhanvantari Nighantu* is the earliest extant medico-botanical dictionary of India. The *Rasaratnakara* of Nagarjuna deals, *inter alia*, with preparations of quicksilver, deemed capable of giving long life, perpetual youth, etc. An advance in the direction of metallic preparations is discerned in the *Chikitsasarasamgraha* of Chakrapandita. His *Sabdachandrika* is a vocabulary of vegetable and mineral substances, and his third work *Dravyagunasamgraha* is a treatise on dietetics. Surapala's (or Suresvara's) *Sabdapradipa* and *Vrikshayurveda* deal with medico-botanical terms and his *Lohapaddhati* discusses the medical use and preparations of iron. The importance of pulse in diagnosis is stressed in Sarngadhara's *Samhita*. The *Hastyayurveda* which deals with the diseases peculiar to elephants, and the *Samhita* of Salihotr, treating the diseases of horses, indicate interest in veterinary science.

Astronomical studies, which began in the Vedic Age, were continued in the *Jyotisha-Vedanga* (c 400 BC). Two great astronomer-cum-mathematicians who might have been born towards the end of the Gupta Age were Bhaskara (I) and Brahmagupta. The latter was the first mathematician to have successfully attempted the solution of the so-called Pellian equation. He was able to state succinctly the rules regarding the volume of a prism, area of a cyclic quadrilateral, and the formula for the length of the two diagonals of a cyclic quadrilateral. Brahmagupta's works played an important part in the introduction among the Arabs of a new mathematics-based astronomy. His treatises, the *Brahmasphuta-Siddhanta* and *Khandakhadyaka*, were translated into Arabic by the eighth century AD. Among the astrological works we can refer to the *Yavana-jataka* of Minaraja. The Gupta Age also provides a landmark in the development of mathematics, astronomy and astrology. Aryabhatta (I), born in 476 AD, the author of the mathematical-astronomical work, *Aryabhatiya*, treated mathematics as a distinct subject and dealt with evolution and involution, area and volume, progressions and algebraic identities, and indeterminate equations of the first degree. His novel alphabetical system of expressing numbers with the help of consonants and vowels was based on the decimal place-value principle.

Astronomy, mathematics and astrology drew attention of a number of talented Indians. Vatesvara, Manjulacharya, Aryabhatta (II), Sripatik, Satananda and Bhaskaracharya made varying contributions to astronomy. The *Laghumanasa* of Manjulacharya introduced into astronomy the corrections due to the precession of the equinoxes. This precession is the sense of retrograde motion and not of oscillation. The precession of the equinoxes was referred to also by Aryabhatta (II), author of the *Aryasiddhanta*. The *Siddhantasiromani* of Bhaskaracharya is an outstanding work of astronomy as well as mathematics. It is remarkable for the lucidity of exposition, depth of treatment, and originality. In several methods and rules relating to arithmetic, geometry and algebra, Indian authors anticipated European scholars of much later ages. Reference can be made to the Rule of Three, and to the arithmetical methods of extracting the square and cube roots of any number (with the knowledge of decimal place-value system), which appeared in Europe not before the fifteenth and sixteenth centuries. In the seventeenth century, W. Snell 'rediscovered' the results achieved much earlier by Brahmagupta while obtaining expressions for the diagonals of quadrilaterals in his study relating to geometry.

Indian genius made great strides in mathematics from an early age, as indicated by archaeological data found at the sites of the Indus Valley civilisation and in Vedic literature. Like the ancient Egyptians, the Vedic mathematicians adopted ten as the basis of numeration, and, unlike the Greeks, were able to think of large numbers in multiples of ten. The knowledge of addition, subtraction, multiplication and division are apparent from several Vedic texts, some of which betray interest in progressive series, both arithmetical and geometrical. Aryabhatta (I) was the first Indian to think of the earth as a sphere and as rotating on its axis, and to observe that eclipse is caused by the shadow of the earth falling on the moon. One of Brahmagupta's results on indeterminate equations was rediscovered about a thousand years later by Euler (1707-1783 AD). His works played an important part in the introduction among the Arabs of a new mathematics-based astronomy.

The Indian mathematical elements, particularly arithmetic, are based on decimal place-value numeration and passed into Latin Europe in the course of transmission of Arabic mathematical knowledge. Algorism or new arithmetic is based on decimal place-value numeration, the knowledge of which reached Europe from India through the Arabic writers. In course of time, this had its impact on the commerce of the Renaissance period, teaching programmes and higher research.

Indians developed some remarkable concepts of the physical world. Among them, we can specially refer to the doctrine of five elements (earth, water, fire or heat, air, and a non-material ubiquitous substance accounting for the diverse world of matter and qualities), the theory of atomism, and knowledge of space, time and motion. The concepts about the physical world continued to be elaborated in the Gupta and post-Gupta periods. Subjects discussed included atomism, motion, heat, light and sound. The Nyaya-Vaiseshika school found out, as indicated by the *Padarthadharma-samgraha* by Prasastapada (c fifth century AD), that gravity is the cause of falling of an object when there is no conjunction or self-reproduction of motion.

Architecture has a long history in India, well attested by archaeology and literary references. It became the subject of full treatises like the *Mayamata, Manasara*, etc. *Vastuvidya* or the Science of Building, i.e. architecture, was a subject of serious concern for the Indians. Substantial progress in civil engineering and technology is evident from the extant remains like mausoleums and mosques, bridges and dams, textiles and ceramics. Mention can be made of the observatories constructed by Sawai Jai Singh II of Jaipur. The astrolabe was the principal instrument for observation. Different types of quadrants and armillary spheres were also utilised. Chemical practices of various kinds are indicated by literary as well as archaeological data. In the second category, we may include the well-known huge metal image of the Buddha from Sultanganj, and the Mehrauli pillar in New Delhi made of wrought iron.

Though railway, telegraph and even photography were introduced in India within a short period of their first use in Europe, study of or research in modern science teaching was in an elementary stage in colleges and laboratories. However, the presence of several European scientists in different capacities in India and their researches brought higher studies in modern science near to the Indians. The last quarter of the nineteenth century witnessed the emergence of eminent personalities like Mahendra Lal Sircar, Asutosh Mukherjee, Jagadish Chandra Bose and Prafulla Chandra Ray, who, among Indians, 'were instrumental in heralding western science teaching and research in India'. Sircar founded the Indian Association for Cultivation of Science, which developed into a centre for training young researchers. Jagadish Chandra Bose (1858-1937) is known for his researches in Electromagnetic waves and responses in plant tissue, which were demonstrated by tools and models, designed and manufactured by him. These contributions to physics and plant physiology were of very high order. Prafulla Chandra Ray (1861-1944), the father of nitrites, pioneered chemical research in modern India and created a band of devoted and successful students who were instrumental in spreading research and teaching in chemistry and allied subjects all over the country. His *History of Hindu Chemistry*, in two volumes, enthused the next generation with the knowledge of our past heritage in science.

C.V. Raman (1888-1970), the inventor of Raman Effect in light scattering, contributed extensively in the realm of light and wave by monitoring the light waves passing through molecules of different elements. Raman's genius was internationally acclaimed when he was awarded the Nobel Prize in 1930. Meghnad Saha (1893-1956) was a pioneer in research in astrophysics. His work on ionization in solar chromosphere and elements in the sun was considered extremely significant. Satyendra Nath Bose ((1894-1974) was an outstanding theoretical physicist who succeeded in deducing Planck's Law of Blackbody Radiation by considering directly the statistics of an assembly of photons in a six-dimensional phase space according to a method which was later extended by Einstein to an assembly of material particles.

Led by the pioneers, Indian scientists and engineers have been studying during the last five decades almost every known aspect of science and technology. Researches of many of them are internationally acclaimed. Dr Homi J. Bhabha played a leading role in putting India on the nuclear map and made her the sixth nation in the world to have harnessed nuclear energy for peaceful purposes. M. Visvesvaraya, Dr Vikram Sarabhai, Dr A.P.J. Abdul Kalam, who is now the President of India, are other scientists and technologists whose researches have brought international fame to the country.

This book, *Science & Technology in India: Twelve Great Scientists*, brings to focus the success stories of some illustrious scientists of India. These stories are not biographical essays in the conventional sense. They are intended to highlight the trials and tribulations these personalities had to face in their efforts to accomplish their objective, and hence convey the message of sincerity, hard work, dedication and the spirit of perseverance to the humanity at large. Their lives point to the need for continued efforts to accomplish our goals, for there are no short cuts to success.

In my efforts, I have been assisted by a number of books from various libraries, particularly that of Jama Millia Islamia University in New Delhi. I am grateful to the University Librarian, Dr Gyas-ud-din Makdooni and his staff members. I would like to thank Rupa & Co for undertaking the publication of this book. My wife, Mrs Asha Ahuja, also deserves my thanks for cooperating with me in my efforts to concentrate on this project. My thanks are also due to various other people who helped me in one way or the other in my endeavours.

5 January 2006   M.L. Ahuja

Vikram Sarabhai

D r Vikram Sarabhai, the scientist, R&D manager, science
and technology policymaker, planner, industrialist, and
the father of India's space programme, was a renaissance
man with interests in music, painting, and architecture. Apart
from devising India's space programme, he defined the role
of scientists and scientific institutions. He not only developed
and launched rockets but also opened the road ahead for us
with new tools and techniques. He was passionately committed
to the use of all aspects of science and technology in general
and space applications in particular as "levers of development",
and as philosophy for organizing and managing scientific
institutions. To him, these were not just the R&D agencies
of atomic energy, space, electronics, CSIR, etc. They were
all organizations in which science and technology was involved.

Sarabhai was born on 12th August 1919 in Ahmedabad.
He was the son of a wealthy businessman, Ambalal Sarabhai
and Saraladevi Sarabhai, who devoted their time and money
to social work. They loved to help the poor and the needy.
They had started a school called "Retreat" for small children,
where children were instructed using toys. Vikram had his

early education in this private school. The school had imaginative teachers, a workshop and an atmosphere of scientific curiosity. New interests at school came to engage Vikram's attention. He was an all-rounder from the beginning. His grasp was quick, his understanding was deep and his memory was sharp. Noticing Vikram's interest in mechanical things, a workshop was added to the school. Vikram spent hours there with the lathes, drills and other machines. Besides making small things, the workshop came to be utilized for carrying out minor repairs. Such occasions gave the future scientist opportunities to exercise his resourcefulness and skill. It also probably inculcated into young Sarabhai the seeds of scientific curiosity, ingenuity and creativity. In high school, Vikram was fascinated with science. Science was like a mystery to him. He became impassioned to discover more. As a young boy, instead of reading storybooks, he used to read about the lives of great scientists. He would spend hours trying to conduct some experiments or just thinking about science.

For his college education, Sarabhai was sent to St. John's College, Cambridge, England, in 1937. Here at the age of eighteen, in the year 1940, he took his Natural Science Tripos with Physics and Mathematics. He studied the latest developments in physics. The outbreak of the Second World War necessitated his return to India. Here, he took up research in cosmic ray physics at the Indian Institute of Science, Bangalore, as a research scholar, working under the inspiring guidance of the Nobel Laureate, Sir C.V. Raman. He chose cosmic rays as his subject and personally built the necessary equipment with which he took measurements at Bangalore, Poona and Apharwat in the Kashmir Himalayas. In Bangalore, he met and married in 1942 Mrinalini Swaminathan, a Bharata Natyam dancer. He encouraged Mrinalini in her dancing career and set up a professional company, Darpana, for her. The couple had a son Kartikeya and a daughter Mallika.

In 1943, Vikram had plans to start a laboratory in Ahmedabad with the help of his friend, Dr K.R. Ramanathan, with interest and reputation in atmospheric physics. Dr Ramanathan was then in the Indian Meteorological Department. He also discussed his plan with other colleagues and friends. He collected a small group of dedicated bright scientists and technicians to start the work. In 1945, when the Second World War ended, he returned to Cambridge and took the PhD degree on his thesis, Cosmic Ray Investigations in Tropical Latitudes. During this period, he also carried out an accurate measurement of the cross-section for the photo-fission of 238U by 6.2 MeV r-rays obtained from the 19F (p,4) reaction. This experiment also formed a part of his PhD thesis which was awarded to him in 1947.

Even as early as 1942, when Dr Sarabhai was working at the Meteorological Department, Poona, he had begun to think of establishing a research laboratory for the study of cosmic rays and atmospheric physics with the help of the then Director of the Poona Observatory. In 1943, as stated above, he went on an expedition to the Himalayan peaks in Kashmir for the measurement of cosmic ray intensities. This experience inspired him to plan a high-altitude research station at a suitable place in Kashmir. Soon after his return from Cambridge, he established the Physical Research Laboratory in Ahmedabad. Professor Ramanathan joined the Laboratory as its first Director in 1948. In this laboratory, he soon began an extensive series of study on cosmic ray time-variations. In 1947, he founded the Ahmedabad Textile Industry's Research Association (ATIRA) of which he was the first Honorary Director, a post which he actively filled till 1956.

It was, in fact, Vikram Sarabhai's interest in cosmic rays together with his passionate zeal that paved the way for the setting up of the Physical Research Laboratory (PRL) at Ahmedabad in November 1947. With the assistance of the Ahmedabad Education Society, the Karmakshetra Educational Foundation as well as Vikram's parents the PRL carried out scientific activities under two broad categories: one under Dr Sarabhai dealing mainly with the time variations of cosmic rays, and the second under Dr Ramanathan in the areas of ionospheric and upper atmospheric physics. Later, a permanent recording station was set up at Ahmedabad and subsequently two more stations were established near the geomagnetic equator at Kodaikanal and Trivandrum which began operations in 1951 and 1955 respectively.

During the years 1950 to 1966, Dr Sarabhai was instrumental in establishing a number of industries in Baroda namely, Sarabhai Chemicals, Sarabhai Glass, Suhrid Geigy Limited, Synbiotics Limited, Sarabhai Merck Limited and the Sarabhai Engineering Group. In Bombay, he took up the management of Swastik Oil Mills, introducing new techniques of oil extraction and the manufacture of synthetic detergents and cosmetics. In Calcutta, he took over the management of Standard Pharmaceuticals Limited where he introduced the large-scale manufacture of Penicillin, besides expanding the range of pharmaceutical products. In 1960, he set up the Sarabhai Research Centre, Baroda, for investigation of natural and synthetic medicinal products. To meet the need of the ever-increasing demand for professional managers in India he founded, in 1962, the Indian Institute of Management in Ahmedabad and was its Honorary Director up to 1965.

With the advent of space research it became possible to check, extend and correlate inferences from earth-bound stations with satellite data. He was quick to take advantage of these opportunities which could give a boost to the interpretation of earth data. He was aware of the fact that this could provide a deep insight into what happens in interplanetary space, the magnetosphere, as well as the sun-earth relationship. A very large meson-detection system was set up at a high altitude laboratory at Chacaltaya, Bolivia, by a group from MIT together with some Japanese workers. Sarabhai quickly seized this opportunity and sent a graduate student there to record and study short-period variations of 1-30 cycles per hour with great accuracy. This led to the discovery of micro pulsations in cosmic ray intensity at the same frequencies as observed in the magnetosphere and interplanetary space by a satellite. A complete correspondence in spectral changes in interplanetary space, magnetosphere and cosmic rays on earth could thus be established.

In 1962, Dr Sarabhai was appointed Chairman of the Indian National Committee for Space Research. He supervised the setting up of the Thumba Equatorial Rocket Launching Station and initiated a programme for the manufacture of French Centaur sounding rockets in India. He was the moving spirit behind the development of rockets of Indian design at Thumba; Rohini and Menaka are among them. In 1966, he was elevated to the post of Chairman of the Atomic Energy Commission and Secretary to the Department of Atomic Energy, Government of India. He was President of the Physics Section of the Indian Science Congress in 1962; Chairman of the Electronics Committee of the Union Department of Defence Supplies and the Electronics Corporation of India Limited, besides being a member of various other important national and international committees. He was a Fellow of the Indian Academy of Science, the National Institute of

Science in India, the Physical Society, London, and the Cambridge Philosophical Society.

Dr Sarabhai drew up plans to take modern education to the remotest villages of India by using satellite television, later implemented as the Satellite Instructional Television Experiment (SITE). His interest in education resulted, in 1965, in his establishing the Community Science Centre, Ahmedabad, for science education for children, an institution where new ideas in science education could be tried out. He also set up the Community Science Centre and the Nehru Foundation for Development. Dr Sarabhai was a member of the International Council of Scientific Unions (1966), Chairman of the Panel of Experts and Scientific Chairman of the UN Conference on the Exploration and Peaceful Uses of Outer Space (1968), President of the 14th General Conference, International Atomic Energy Agency, Vienna (1970), and Vice-President of Fourth UN Conference on the Peaceful Uses of Atomic Energy (1971).

In recognition of his contribution towards science, Dr Sarabhai was awarded the Shanti Swaroop Bhatnagar Memorial Award for Physics in 1962. He was also decorated with the Padma Bhushan in 1966 by the Government of India; the Padma Vibhushan was awarded to him posthumously. He died on 30 December 1971 while he was on a visit to Thumba Equatorial Rocket Launching Station in Trivandrum.

It was science writer Arthur C. Clarke who first envisaged the feasibility of a communication satellite in a geosynchronous orbit hovering 36,800 km above the earth but stationary in relation to the earth. This would make possible quick and efficient telephone links between countries, cities and villages. Even in 1965, when very few such geosynchronous satellites were up in orbit, Dr Sarabhai pioneered a new concept for the developing world by using such a satellite not only for communication but also for community education. This resulted in the famous Indian SITE programme under which 2400 villages were hooked up with TSV through the ATS-F.

Dr Vikram Sarabhai lived the life of a karma yogi, performing his self-allotted duties: swadharma with selfless (anasakta) and tireless devotion. He used to come up with almost a dozen ideas a day. Although he knew that most of them were speculative or unrealistic, still he went on in his quest of scientific inquiry. Maybe that was his way to keep up his mental agility and sharpen his perceptiveness. Above all, he was a warm, humane personality, ever modest, deeply simple in his ways, soft-spoken and courteous. He worked right up to the end with an urgency which had to be seen to be believed, working against time, as if he knew he had so much to accomplish in so little time.

He was a visionary much ahead of time. Consequently, he expected his team to look towards the future. When his team would be already working on one project, Dr Sarabhai would unroll his ideas on the development of another project. Thus, the first indigenous sounding rocket was launched through his initiatives followed by the designing of a satellite launch vehicle. He taught his colleagues how to dream. He piloted efforts on space, earth resources, meteorology and, above all, on raising the technological base of the country as a whole. Today, we have visible proof of the soundness of his long-range perspective. It is a remarkable tribute to his foresight that, over the years since his untimely death, there has never been an occasion to deviate from the space programme profile delineated by Sarabhai as far back as 1970. The faith he reposed in the scientific community of India has ensured the continuity of the technological leadership that we have today.

Robert Frost wrote: "....I have promises to keep....And miles to go before I sleep...." Vikram Sarabhai, too, in his short life span achieved numerous landmarks before bidding us adieu. With his infinite capacity for hard work, he always worked more than eighteen to twenty hours a day, advocating as well as practising 'stretch your working hours when you feel overburdened'. Vikram Sarabhai demonstrated in his very short span of life that dreams could be realized if you have the will.

Sushruta

Sushruta is generally considered as the greatest ancient surgeon that India has produced. He is believed to be the disciple of Dhanvantari and is credited for elevating the art of handling a lancet or forceps to the status of a practical science. His *Sushruta Samhita* deals with the problems of practical surgery and midwifery. He is known to be of the race of Vishvamitra. The *Mahabharata* represents him as a son of that royal sage. The *Garuda Puranam* places Divodasa, fourth in descent from Dhanvantari, as the first to propound medical science on earth, whereas the *Sushruta Samhita* describes the two as identical persons. But this apparent anomaly in the *Samhita* can be explained by the popular practice of attaching one's father's name or that of a glorious ancestor to one's name for better identification. It is, therefore, not surprising that Divodasa (the preceptor of Sushruta), who was a firm believer in the doctrine of psychic transmigration, should represent himself as an incarnation of Dhanvantari, and assume his name and style in the usual way.

It is believed that Sushruta lived sometime during the latter part of the fourth century before the Christian era and the original *Sushruta Samhita* must have been written at least two centuries earlier in order to acquire that hoary authority and prescription of age. The general consensus of expert opinion is to place Charaka prior to Sushruta in respect of time. But the Puranas unanimously describe Sushruta as a disciple of Dhanvantari, the first propounder of medical science.

Sushruta Samhita deals, *inter alia*, with preliminary surgical measures; characteristic features of the different seasons of the year and their influence on health and drugs; surgical appliances and instruments; teaching of surgery on dummies and suitable fruits; essential qualifications of a physician before he formally enters his profession; leeches and their use; features of lymph chyle; piercing and bandaging of the lobules of ears; dressings and bandages of ulcers, nursing and management of an ulcer patient and secretions from boils and ulcers; eight different forms of surgical operation; extraction of splinters; clinical observations, drugs, modes of administering emetics, choice of purgatives; diseases of the nervous system, haemorrhoids, urinary callculii; diseases of the urinary tract; diseases affecting mammary glands of women; fracture and dislocation, etc.; anatomy, purification of semen and cataminal fluid etc.; pregnancy, nursing and management of pregnant women, development of factors in the womb; anatomy of the human body, vital parts of the body, etc.; description of the arteries, nerves and ducts; medical treatment of fractures; treatment of snake-bites, rat-poisoning etc.; diagnosis and treatment of eyes, ear diseases, nasal diseases, fever, diarrhoea, heart disease, jaundice, haemorrhage, fainting fits, vomiting, cough, asthma, defects of urine, insanity, etc.

According to Chapter 1 of *Sushruta Samhita*, when the holy Dhanvantari, the greatest of the mighty celestials, incarnated in the form of Divodasa, the king of Kasi, was blissfully seated in his hermitage, surrounded by a concourse of holy *Rishis*, Sushruta and others requested him to illuminate their minds with the truths of eternal Ayurveda (medical science) to alleviate the sufferings of mankind. The self-begotten Brahma strung it together into a hundred thousand couplets (*shlokas*), divided into one thousand chapters.

The whole of Ayurveda was divided into eight different branches: the *Salya-Tantrum, Shalakya-Tantram, Kaya-Chikitsa, Bhuta-Vidya, Kaumara-Bhritya, Agada-Tantram, Rasayana-Tantram* and *Vajeekarana-Tantram*. The scope of *Salya-Tantram* is to remove from an ulcer any extraneous substance such as fragments of hay, particles of stone, dust, iron or bone, splinters, nails, hair, clotted blood, or condensed pus. The *Shalakya-Tantram* is concerned with the treatment of those diseases which are restricted to the upward fissures or cavities of the body, such as the ears, eyes, the cavity of the mouth, nostrils, etc. The *Kaya-Chikitsa* treats diseases which affect the entire system like fever, dysentery, etc. The *Bhuta-Vidya* lays down incantations and modes of exorcising evil spirits and making offerings to the gods, demons, etc. The *Kaumara-Bhritya* deals with the nursing and healthy upbringing of infants. The *Agada-Tantram* deals with bites from snakes, spiders and venomous worms. The *Rasayana-Tantram* has the object of the prolongation of human life, and the invigoration of memory and vital organs. The *Vajeekarana-Tantram* offers measures by which the semen of a man naturally scanty or deficient in quality becomes shorn of its defects.

Vedic India, like ancient Egypt, recognised the principle of division of labour among the followers of the healing art. There were *Shalya Vaidyas* (surgeons), *Bhisaks* (physicians) and *Bhisagatharvans* (magic doctors), and at the time of the

Mahabharata, which nearly approached the age of Sushruta, the number of sects had increased to five: *Rogahargas* (physicians), *Shalyaharas* (surgeons), *Visharas* (poison-curers), *Krityaharas* (demon-doctors) and *Bhisag-Atharvans* (magic doctors). In the Vedic age (before the age of Sushruta) physicians had to go out into the open streets, calling out for patients. They lived in houses surrounded by gardens containing medicinal herbs. Verses eulogising the virtues of water as an all-healer, and of certain trees and herbs as purifiers of the atmosphere, are not uncommon in the Vedas. Indeed, the rudiments of embryology, midwifery, child management (paediatrics) and sanitation were formulated in the age of the Vedas and Brahmanas.

In India, as in all other countries, curative spells and healing *mantras* preceded medicine. The first man of medicine in India was a priest, a *Bhisag-Atharvan*, who held a superior position to a surgeon in society. In fact, surgery originally lent its aid materially towards the healing up of traumatic ulcers. Ulcers incidental to blows and sword-cuts had to be dressed and attended to in the wars between the gods and the demons, long before the appearance of any physical or idiopathic maladies such as fever, and surgery contributed to the healing of those ulcers. Hence, it is the oldest of all the allied branches of the healing art. In the Rig Veda, we find that legs were amputated and replaced by iron substitutes, injured eyes were plucked out, and arrow shafts were extracted from the limbs of the Aryan warriors. Many difficult surgical operations seemed to have been successfully carried out. Though the aid of surgery was constantly sought for, surgeons were not often allowed to mix in the Brahmanic society of Vedic India. Over a period of time, surgeons were no longer required in camps and on battlefields. They had only to attend on the rich ladies at baronial castles during parturition; the magic doctor

(*Bhisag-Atarvan*) could assuage fever and concoct love potions. To Sushruta goes the credit of systematically arranging the surgical experience of the older surgeons, and of collecting the scattered facts of the science from the vast range of Vedic literature.

Practical surgery requires good knowledge of anatomy. The quartered animals at the Vedic sacrifices afforded excellent materials for the framing of a comparative anatomy. Sushruta devoted his whole life to the pursuit of proper surgery, to which he brought a mind stored with luminous analogies from the lower animals. It was he who first classified all surgical operations into eight different kinds, and grouped them under *Aharya* (extraction of solid bodies), *Bhedya* (excising), *Chhedyya* (incising), *Eshya* (probing), *Lekhya* (scarifying), *Sivya* (suturing), *Vedhya* (puncturing) and *Visravaniya* (evacuating fluids). The system of surgery devised by Sushruta recognises 125 different surgical instruments constructed after the shape of beasts and birds, and authorises the surgeon to devise new instruments according to the requirements of each case.

The qualifications and equipments of a surgeon are practically the same as are recommended at the present time. Light refreshment is enjoined to be given to the patient before a surgical operation, while abdominal operations and operations in the mouth are advised to be performed while the patient is fasting. Sushruta enjoins the sick room to be fumigated with the vapours of white mustard, *Nimva* leaves, and resinous gums of *Shala* trees, etc. which foreshadows the antiseptic (bacilli) theory of modern times. The number of surgical devices described in the *Samhita* is decidedly small in comparison with the almost inexhaustible resources of Western surgery, and one may be led to suspect the authenticity of the glorious achievements claimed by the surgeons of yore.

Their knowledge of the properties and virtues of drugs was so great that cases, which are reckoned as surgical nowadays, were cured with the help of internally applied medicines. Surgery was only employed when the affected vital energy was not strong enough to alone effect the cure. According to the *Samhita*, ophthalmic, obstetric and other operations were performed with utmost skill and caution.

According to Dr Hirschberg of Berlin, 'plastic surgery in Europe took a new flight when these curing devices of Indian workmen became known to us.' The transplanting of sensible skin-flaps is also an entirely Indian method. It is Sushruta who first successfully demonstrated the feasibility of mending a clipped earlobe with a patch of sensible skin-flap scraped from the neck or the adjoining part. To Sushruta is attributed the glory of discovering the art of cataract-crouching, which was unknown to the surgeons of ancient Greece and Egypt. Limbs were amputated, abdominal sections were performed, fractures were set, dislocations, hernia and ruptures were reduced, haemorrhoids and fistula were removed, and the methods recommended in the *Sushruta Samhita* proved more successful than those adopted by modern-day surgeons. In the case where the intestines are injured, Sushruta advises that 'the protruded part should be gently replaced by following with the finger.' He wants the surgeon to enlarge the wound in it, if necessary, by means of a knife. In the case where the intestine is severed, the severed parts should be held together by applying living black ants to their ends. Then their bodies should be cut off leaving only the heads to serve the same purpose, which, in modern improved European surgery, an animal tissue like catgut is expected to fulfil. After this, the intestine should be fairly replaced in the abdominal cavity and the external opening stitched and properly dressed. Certain medicinal plasters were applied to localise the shafts of arrows embedded in the limbs of wounded soldiers and their exact locations were ascertained from the inflammation caused by the application of plaster with a precision which would be sometimes welcome even in these days of Rontgen rays.

Sushruta enjoins that the stone, if in the urethra, should be removed with the help of *Anuvisanam* and urethral enemata, failing which the penis should be cut open and the concretion extracted with the help of a hook. Amputations were freely made and medicated wines were given to the patients as anaesthetics. All this demonstrates that the surgery of Sushruta does not rest content with the mere bursting or opening of an abscess and the healing of the incidental wound, but lays down processes for major operations as well. He has laid down norms for ophthalmic surgery. Of the 76 varieties of ophthalmic diseases, Sushrata holds that 51 are surgical. The mode of operation to be performed in each case has been elaborately described in the *Samhita*. He was aware of the fact that the angle of reflection is equal to the angle of incidence, and that the same ray which impinges upon the retina, serves the double purpose of illumining the eye and the external world, and is in itself converted into the sensation of light.

Sushruta's greatness is evident in the sphere of practical midwifery. The different turning, flexing, gliding movements, the application of the forceps in cases of difficult labour and other obstetric operations involving the destruction and mutilation of the child, such as craniotomy, were first systematically described in the *Sushruta Samhita* long before fillets and forceps were thought of in Europe. He advocates caesarean section in hopeless cases of obstruction and lays down that the instrument should be employed only in those cases where the proportion between the child and the maternal passage is so defective that medicated plasters, fumigation, etc. are not sufficient to effect a natural delivery. His directions regarding the management of the puerperal state, lactation and management of the child and the choice of wet-nurse are substantially the same as are found in modern scientific works of European authors.

He was the first to advocate the dissection of dead bodies as indispensable for a successful student of surgery. He said, 'Theory without practice is like a one-winged bird that is incapable of flight.' To gain efficiency in surgical operations, he asked his pupils to try their knives repeatedly, first on natural and artificial objects resembling the diseased parts of the body, before undertaking an actual operation. Incision, for example, was practised on *Pushpafala* (*Cucerbeta maxima*), *Alavu* (*Longenaris vulgaris*) or *Trapusha* (*Cucmis pubescuas*), evacuating on leather bags full of water and on the urinary bladders of dead animals, scarification on the hides of animals on which the hair was allowed to remain. The art of stuffing and probing on bamboo reeds, etc. was learnt through extraction of solid bodies on *Panasa* (*Artocarpus integrifolia*) and such fruits. Scraping was done on wax spread on a *Shalmali* (*Bombox malabaricum*) plank, and suturing on pieces of cloth, skin or hide. Ligaturing and bandaging were practised on dummies, cauterisation (both actual and potential) on pieces of flesh, and catheterisation on unbaked earthen vessels filled with water. The quartered sacrificial animals afforded excellent materials for the framing of comparative anatomy.

Sushruta discusses the question, what is man, wherein lies his individuality, why does he come into being, why does he die at all? Like all Indian philosophers, Sushruta argues the question down from the universe to man. The factors or laws governing the evolution of the universe in its physical aspect are extended to cover the evolution of the physical aspect of man (organic evolution). There is but one law and one force which runs through the three domains of mind, matter and spirit. Physiology, that fails to look into the nature of life and its background and tries to explain away this intelligent, living force as the product of chemical action of the organic cells, is no physiology at all. He explained that cell is not life, but there is life in a cell.

Some light is thrown on the relative preponderance of the sperm and ovum in the birth of a female child. It is explained that when the maternal element preponderates, the child is female. When the paternal element is stronger the child is male. When both the elements are equal, the child has no sex. In theory at least, Sushruta admits the possibility of the birth of many children at a single conception. When the seed is divided into two by its inherent force (*Vayu*), twins are born in the womb, a statement which points to the irresistible conclusion that multiplicity of birth is the outcome of the multifarious fission of the seed in the womb under certain abnormal conditions. Sushruta gives a reason for believing that in exceptional circumstances and without sexual union, the unfertilised ovum may give rise to a perfect offspring, thus giving a prevision of the modern theory of parthenogenesis. He extends the probability to the human ova under certain conditions. He admits the possibility of conception without the admixture of the male germinal element, though he observes that like all asexual genesis the development does not proceed far in the case. From such a hypothesis it is but one step to the theory which enunciates the possibility of conception without proper sexual union. Sushruta lays down rules of diet and conduct to be observed by the enceinte, from month to month, during the whole period of gestation, and gives medicinal recipes for the development of a partially atrophied child in the womb.

The Vedic physicians possessed at least a considerable knowledge of the process of digestion, the circulation of gas in the human organism, and of the properties and functions of flesh, fat, muscles, tendons, ligaments and cartilages. But to the Acharyas of the Ayurveda belongs the glory of first formulating a systematic physiological science, to which end Sushruta as a surgeon did contribute no mean a quota. According to Western science, the actions of living matter may be reduced to three categories: (a) sustentative, (b) generative, and (c) correlative. Sushruta observes some such distinction among the functions of a living organism when he denominates the living body as the 'the three supported one' (*Tristhunam*), and describes the normal *Vayu*, *Pittam* and *Kapham* as its three supports. *Vayu*, according to Sushruta, is so called from the fact of its sensory and motor functions such as smelling, etc.

What is it in a man, asks Sushruta, which falls sick? What is it that we treat medicinally—the body or the mind? Sushruta says that 'anything that afflicts the inner man (self or *Purusha*) is disease and that disease has its primary seat in the inner spring of vitality from which it flows out to the surface, the external body'. In man, as in everything else in the universe, the direction of the inherent force is from the centre to the circumference. The shock is felt first at the centre of vitality, from where it is transmitted outwards and thus affects the energy which holds the molecules together, *Dvyanuks* and *Tryanuks* (binary and tertiary atoms) of which the gross body is composed, and further opposes the dissolution of those molecules into their elemental constituents in the living organism. Even in cases of external injuries, such as snake-bite, the potency of the virus is carried at once to the centre from where it is almost instantaneously transmitted through the external channels of the body to its surface. Otherwise what purpose does *vayu* (nerve force) serve in the human anatomy? In all diseases, the subjective sensations are the first to be experienced. 'I am ill', 'I feel hot', etc. are the voices of sensations, which form the essence of the disease. Disease then is a force and not matter.

Sushruta observes that the relation between a disease and the deranged *Vayu* (nerve force), *Pittam* (metabolism) and *Kapham* (unutilised product of the system), and the pathogenic factors which lie at the root of that disease, is not real but contingent. These morbific principles may permeate the whole organism without creating any discomfort, and it is only when they find a distinct lodgement and are centred in some distinct part or tissue of the body, that they become the exciting factors of disease. And what is medicine and is it in the drug that cures? Sushruta, after closely investigating all the theories on the subject, inclines towards the opinion that it is the potency of the drug that is curative though he observes that potency cannot exist independently of all drugs. A drug is of primary interest for all practical purposes in therapy. The potency is administered best when the physical or chemical properties of a drug are annihilated. This is best performed by subjecting it to heat or pressure. Sushruta emphasises the value of psychopathy in mental or nervous distempers.

Powders, decoctions, as well as medicated oils, *Ghritas*, confection and wines are some of the forms in which, according to Sushruta, medicines should be given. The different drugs, such as roots, leaves, etc. should be culled in the seasons proper to each. He classifies soil into five different kinds for the purpose of growing drugs having different therapeutic properties. Even the virtues of different flavours and colours were ascertained with regard to their respective actions on the deranged morbific principles of the body. A good and proper diet in disease is worth a hundred medicines and no amount of medication can do good to a patient who does not observe a strict regimen of diet, laid down Sushruta.

Sushruta divides the whole vegetable kingdom into four groups: *Vriksha, Gulma, Vanaspati* and *Virudha*. His botany is in the nature of a *Materia Medica*. He mentions the habitat and describes the foliage of certain plants so that they may be distinguished from others of a cognate species. He describes the methods of preparing oxides, sulphates or chlorides of the six metals as the case may be. Processes for the preparation of alkalis and the lixiviation of ashes are very elaborately described. As a writer of hygiene and public health, he emphasises the importance of cleanliness of both spirit and body. Water is the subject of discussion of an entire chapter in the *Samhita*. Outbreaks of epidemics have been attributed to contrary seasons, to the floating of minute particles of poisonous flower pollen in the air, and to the sin or unrighteous conduct of the community. Earthquakes, famines, and other physical phenomena, which are, at present, attributed to magnetic disturbances of the earth, have been described by him as the usual precursors of devastating epidemics such as plague.

It is a fundamental dictum of Sushruta that in a case of medical treatment, the then prevailing season of the year should be taken into account. In his *Samhita*, we find two distinct classifications of seasons. One is based on the peculiar physical phenomena which distinguish the different seasons of the year, a fact which emphatically proves that Sushruta was an inhabitant of the sub-Himalayan Gangetic Doab. The other classification is for the purpose of showing the respective accumulation, aggravation and subsidence of morbific diatheses (*Doshas*). In the same manner, the different quarters of the day and night have been minutely charted to show the spontaneous aggravation and subsidence of the deranged *Vayu*, *Pittam* and *Kapham* during the twenty-four hours. The influence of planets in producing certain diseases like smallpox, measles, scarlet fever, etc. is almost a proven fact. The vegetable kingdom from which we glean our daily food is also subject to this influence.

For the treatment of the diseases of kidney, bladder and the urethra, Sushruta has described the symptoms and the colour of the urine in each specific variety without laying down any mode of testing the urine. In the section *Kalpasthanam* of the *Samhita*, he has described the symptoms of hydrophobia and snakebites, etc. as well as those developed in cases of vegetable poisoning, together with their therapeutic treatment and remedies. It has been lately discovered by a German physiologist that tubercular bacilli do not thrive in goat's blood. The importance of goat's milk in colitis as an efficient agent in checking ferment in the intestines, or of the close contact of a goat as a powerful auxiliary in curing tuberculous phthisis, was first demonstrated by Sushruta.

It is, therefore, safer to conclude that Sushruta was the pioneer in medicine the world over. Solon (638-558 BC), Pythagoras (580-498 BC) and Philostratus (3rd century BC) have all acknowledged that even the ancient Egyptians, to whom the Greeks were to a great extent indebted for their own culture and civilisation, 'obtained much of their knowledge from some mysterious nation of the East' (Wise, 1845). The work of Sushruta is one of the greatest of its kind in Sanskrit literature. It is especially important from the surgical point of view, for he was the first to elevate the art of surgery into a practical science during the remote Vedic period.

Aryabhatta

*T*he launching of 'Aryabhatta' by the Indian Space Research Organisation (ISRO) into space on 19 April 1973 not only secured for India the eleventh position in space research, it also focussed attention on the inimitable contributions of the author of *Aryabhatiya*, in whose memory the satellite was named. Aryabhatta, whose 1500th birth centenary was celebrated by the Indian National Science Academy in New Delhi on 2 November 1976, is regarded as the father of Indian astronomy and is also known for his contributions to mathematics. Dedicated to Lord Brahma, the creator of this universe, Aryabhatta pursued astronomy and mathematics as he thought that his findings in these subjects would enable him to understand fully the universe created by his Lord. He holds a unique position in the galaxy of Indian mathematicians and astronomers whose works have been studied through the ages like scriptures.

The Muslim historian, Al-Biruni, has mentioned that there were two Aryabhattas. The elder was known as Aryabhatta I, while the other was called Aryabhatta II. Al-Biruni has maintained that the latter followed the doctrines of the former.

But it is the author of *Aryabhatiya* who is credited with the enormous contributions in the fields of astronomy and mathematics. There are also two opinions about Aryabhatta's date of birth. Some say he was born on 21 March 476 AD while others believe it to be 13 April 476 AD. He lived in Kusumpura identified with Patna, the capital of Bihar, on the Ganges. The Bihar Research Society, Patna, celebrates his birth anniversary on 13 April every year. It was during Aryabhatta's time that the Indian intellect reached its high watermark in most branches of arts, science and literature.

No authentic information is available regarding the life of Aryabhatta. Even the *Aryabhatiya* does not throw light on such aspects as his parentage, his educational career, or other details of his personal life. From the writings of Bhaskara I, who belonged to his school, it appears that Aryabhatta took up the profession of a teacher. He earned a name as a great scholar and teacher of astronomy. He has been referred to as *Acharya* (Professor) and *Sarva-Sidhhanta Guru* by Bhaskara I. He has also been designated as *Kulpa* which means *Kulapati* (Vice-Chancellor) of the University of Nalanda, which was one of the premier centres of learning in the country at that time.

According to some historians, Aryabhatta was the first great scientist, astronomer and mathematician of ancient India. Before him there were many great *rishis* who made mathematical contributions to the Vedas and the *Sulva Sutras*. The seven *Sulva Sutras* were named after seven great *rishis*, but these were essentially religious works, in which mathematics came in because of the need for the construction of altars, while mathematics and astronomy together got included because of the need to determine the auspicious time for religious rituals. Aryabhatta also approached the subject in a religious spirit, but in a different manner.

Aryabhatta was a great devotee of Lord Brahma, the creator of the universe. Myth has it that Lord Brahma, who was pleased with his great devotion, revealed the knowledge contained in the *Aryabhatiya* to him. This may or may not be true, but his devotion to Lord Brahma inspired him to find out the truth about the universe created by the Lord. In his view, the goal of all learning was the attainment of the Supreme One and this could easily be achieved through astronomy. Since mathematics was needed in order to understand astronomy, it was also very important. He looked at mathematics and astronomy as the means to a much higher goal. This was different from the earlier attitude, namely, that mathematics was needed for the construction of altars and that mathematics and astronomy were subservient to astronomy for finding auspicious *mahurats* for rituals to propitiate gods and goddesses. His attitude was that it was necessary to investigate the truth about Nature in order to know the truth about its Creator. He maintained that the end of learning was the attainment of the supreme Brahma and this could easily be done through the study of astronomy. He acknowledged the grace of Brahma on the successful completion of his book, *Aryabhatiya*, in one of the closing stanzas. This shows his deep devotion to Brahma, and this has led some to believe that Aryabhatta acquired his knowledge of astronomy by performing penance in propitiation of Lord Brahma. It is said that Aryabhatta followed exactly in the footsteps of Vyasa, the son of Parasara, the 'ornament among men', who, 'by virtue of penance, acquired the knowledge of the subjects beyond the reach of the senses and the poetic eye capable of (doing) good to others.' He believed that one, who knows the motion of the earth and the planets on the celestial sphere after piercing through the orbit of the planets and the stars, attains the supreme Brahma—the path of salvation.

Aryabhatta's predilection for the Brahma school of astronomy might have been inspired by two main considerations. Firstly, the Brahma school was the most ancient school of Hindu astronomy promulgated by Lord Brahma himself. Secondly, the astronomers of Kusumpura, where Aryabhatta lived and wrote his *Aryabhatiya*, were the followers of that school. He is also credited with a number of pupils. Pandurangaswami, Latadeva and Nisenku are believed to have learnt astronomy from him.

He believed in investigation and established new values of astronomical parameters by careful observation. He studied the available literature and found many mathematical and astronomical results scattered in various religious books. A careful study was made, gaps were filled, and errors corrected. He felt the need for writing a textbook and consolidating the knowledge. He did not prove his results in the tradition of Greek mathematics, but gave them in compact form in the Indian tradition. In just 33 *shlokas* dealing with mathematics, he considered geometrical figures and their properties, mensuration, interest series, simultaneous and quadratic equations, linear indeterminate equations, square roots, cube roots, method of constructing sine tables, etc. Similarly, in just 50 *shlokas* the motion of the sun, the moon and the planets on the celestial sphere were dealt with. He described the various circles on this sphere and indicated the method of automatically rotating the sphere once in twenty-four hours to explain the motion of the Earth, sun, moon and planets. He has also explained the methods of finding the length of the Earth's shadow. Multiply the distance of the sun from the Earth by the diameter of the Earth and divide (the product) by the difference between the diameters of the sun and the Earth. The result is the length of the shadow of the Earth, he explained. What is called shadow, he said, is darkness caused by the Earth's shadow. The moon eclipses the sun and the great shadow of the Earth eclipses the moon. In this process, when at the end of a lunar month, the moon lying near its node, enters the Earth's shadow, it is more or less the middle of an eclipse, a solar eclipse in the former case and a lunar eclipse in the latter case.

One of the greatest theories of Aryabhatta concerns the motion of the Earth, its shape, size and other aspects. Because of this unorthodox theory, Aryabhatta was the subject of criticism for a long time. People could not, in fact, understand his theory about the Earth. Even at that time, he knew that the Earth was round and not flat. It shines due to the sun. He wrote that the globe of the Earth stands in space at the centre of the circular frame of the asterisms, surrounded by the orbits. It is made of water, earth, fire and air, and is spherical. Further, he not only talked about the space of the Earth, but also of its construction. He maintained that the Earth is not stationary but moves around the sun. Just as a man, he wrote, sitting in a boat going forward, sees a stationary object moving backward, so at Lanka, a hypothetical place of O (zero) latitude and longitude, the immovable stars appear to move westward. The structure of the asterisms is stationary. It is the Earth itself which, making a rotation every day, causes the rising and setting of the stars and planets. He worked on the motion and position of different planets. He said that a true planet moved in eccentric circles or in epicycles and the radius of a planet's epicycle is the same as the distance between the centre of the planets, eccentric circle and the Earth. According to Aryabhatta, the planet which is situated on the circumference of its epicycle moves with its mean velocity.

Aryabhatta produced at least three works on astronomy— *Aryabhatiya, Aryabhatta-Siddhanta* and *Surya-Siddhanta-*

Prakasa. The first one is well known, while the second and third works are known only through references to them in later works. The *Aryabhatiya* deals both with mathematics and astronomy. In this, he was much inspired by the available literature and, wherever necessary, corrected and modified the erroneous results. The work contains astronomical parameters based on his observations. He wrote the first edition at the age of twenty-three and the work was revised later on. It is considered an excellent textbook on astronomy due to the brevity and conciseness of expression, superiority of astronomical content, and innovations in astronomical methods. It gave birth to a new school of astronomy, the Aryabhatta School, of which Bhaskara I was the most illustrious student. The book is also considered as a popular work on ancient mathematics. Aryabhatta was probably the first astronomer who gave a table of sine differences. He had also stated geometrical and theoretical methods for constructing sine tables. He did not believe in the theory of creation and annihilation of the world. He was of the opinion that time was a continuous process without beginning and end. The beginnings of *yuga* and *kalpa*, he believed, have nothing to do with any terrestrial occurrence. They are based purely on astronomical phenomena, depending on the position of the planets in the sky. He rejected the highly artificial scheme of time division prevailing at that time and replaced it with the following:

One day of Brahma or *Kalpa* = 14 *manus*;
One *manu* = 72 *yugas*;
One *yuga* = 43,20,000 years

In the 33 *shlokas* of the *Aryabhatiya* he deals with square root, cube root, areas of different geometric shapes, right-angled triangles, quadratic equations, indeterminate equations of first order and other topics of mathematics. The most important of the different branches of mathematics are the rules for performing arithmetic operations according to the decimal place-value numeration. He was the first Indian mathematician to adopt the decimal place-value system and to write formally on mathematics. He gave a number of new results in arithmetic. He is also called the father of algebra in India. His contributions in the field of equations and their solutions are enormous. He introduced the rules to solve some other types of indeterminate problems. He is also credited for developing the theory of the indeterminate equation, of the first degree in algebra, the value of η correct to four decimal places, the methods of computing the sine table in trigonometry and the theory of the Earth's rotation in astronomy. It is also Aryabhatta who laid the foundation of the so-called *Siddhantic* astronomy and provided it with new tools and techniques, more accurate parameters, and better methods of observation and computation. His *Aryabhatta-Siddhanta* was a popular work and was used not only as a textbook of astronomy but also in everyday calculations, such as those pertaining to marriage, nativity, etc. Not much is known about his third work *Surya-Siddhanta-Prakash*.

To conclude, Aryabhatta was a great pioneer in mathematics and astronomy. His research findings not only inspired his contemporaries, but have also facilitated further research for the succeeding generations. His works influenced the Arabs who spread them to other parts of the world. He was the first to develop epicyclic astronomy. He discovered the causes of eclipses and the scientific method of calculating the time of their occurrence. If Kalidasa is the Shakespeare of India, Valmiki the Indian Homer, Aryabhatta may be called the Indian Newton. He developed Indian astronomy without the aid of telescope or spectroscope and other astronomical instruments. It was his genius that led him to discuss mathematics and astronomy as separate disciplines, thereby allowing mathematics to develop rapidly in the succeeding centuries. In that sense, he can be called the 'father of astronomy and mathematics' in India.

Jagadish Chandra Bose

The Bose Institute in Kolkata, devoted to important research work in areas as different as theoretical physics and biotechnology, reflects the wide interests of the founder, the great scientist and versatile genius, Sir Jagadish Chandra Bose. Though he is famous for his research in electromagnetic waves and responses in plant tissue, Bose was also an accomplished scholar specialising in various fields. He was an ardent nationalist, and his versatile genius found expression in literary works also. The Bose Institute continues with the legacy of its illustrious founder by doing pioneering work in the physical and natural sciences.

Jagadish Chandra Bose was the son of Bhagwan Chandra Bose, a courageous and enterprising officer in the British Raj. Born on 30 November 1858 at Mymensingh, in what is now Bangladesh, Jagadish belonged to a humble family. His father, Bhagwan Chandra, often fought with dacoits. Once he even single-handedly caught a dacoit. Jagadish studied in the local *pathshala* (school) of Faridpur (now in Bangladesh) and later in St Xavier's School in Calcutta (now Kolkata). His classmates were children of the local farm labourers, farmers, fishermen and petty shopkeepers. From them he developed his love for equality, justice, fair play and brotherhood. From them he also got inspired about trees, mountains and rivers. He accompanied his father to the neighbouring jungles. All this inspired in him love for Nature and the universe. The boy became curious to know many things and they became subjects of his research, finally making him a scholar and a scientist.

When Jagadish's father, Bhagwan Chandra, was elevated to the position of Assistant Commissioner in Burdwan he set up the Technical Training School in the compound of his own bungalow to groom the rural youth for the development of industries. The school was equipped with a machine shop and a foundry. This exposed Jagadish to machines and technicians. He himself learnt the basic skills in carpentry, grinding, welding, moulding, etc. The skills he acquired subsequently stood him in good stead in designing and building sensitive instruments.

At the age of sixteen, Jagadish joined St Xaviers College, Calcutta. In this college, Father Lafont, a Christian missionary and astronomer, inspired him. Father Lafont always used novel methods of teaching science through experiments and questions. Jagadish was keen to become a physicist, but his parents could not afford to send him to England for further study. His mother sold her jewellery to finance her son's trip to England for the study of medicine. The foul air in the dissecting rooms affected Jagadish's health. He had to abandon his medical studies. In 1881, he shifted to science and joined Christ's College, Cambridge. In 1884, he passed the Natural Science Tripos of Cambridge University and had his BS degree from London University. His teachers happened to be renowned scientists like Lord Rayleigh, Michael Foster, Francis Darwin and Sidney Vines, among others.

In 1885, when he was twenty-seven, Jagadish Chandra Bose returned to India. He joined the then Imperial Service of the British Empire. He was appointed a professor of physics in Presidency College, Calcutta. He was the first Indian to adorn this post. It was at a time when the British rulers treated Indians as an inferior race with no inclination for science and experimentation. Even a most qualified Indian was not considered good enough to teach a difficult subject like physics. Thus, the appointment of Jagadish Chandra Bose raised eyebrows in the British circle. Brought up in a different environment where equality, justice and brotherhood were valued, the new ambience hurt his sentiments. He decided to show his protest against this discrimination by refusing to draw his salary, though he continued to teach his students with great enthusiasm and interest.

He got married to Abala. The family had difficult days. It even became difficult for Bose to manage the basic household expenses. His father, however, supported his son in his fight against racial discrimination and injustice. He urged him to follow the footsteps of Karna, one of the heroes of the epic *Mahabharata*. His father inculcated in him the spirit of indomitable courage, of conviction to face the vicissitudes in life. His teachings became a source of inspiration for the son, and the young man devoted himself to the arduous task of scientific research. For three years, Bose continued teaching at the college without taking his salary. He was a popular teacher. He endeared himself to his students with his innovative and delectable ways of teaching. He also conducted research in a small room allotted to him in the college. The British authorities ultimately felt impressed with his art of teaching and at last Bose consented to accept his full salary right from the day he had joined the college. He now had immense faith in his ability to face challenges.

Though the British physicist James Clerk Maxwell demonstrated the existence of radio waves, and the German physicist Heinrich Hertz produced them in 1887, the experiments on wireless telegraphy were successfully conducted by Jagadish Chandra Bose in 1894. Oliver Lodge's book, *Heinrich Hertz and His Successors* fascinated him. On studying the book, he started experiments on wireless telegraphy in a small room allotted to him in his college laboratory. Using his own money, he modified devices and materials found after much searching in scrap shops with the assistance of an illiterate tinsmith. He built the equipment needed for the generation of radio waves. He designed and fabricated a new type of 'radiator' for generating radio waves and also a unique and highly sensitive 'coherer' or radio receiver to catch them. His radio receiver consisted of spiral strings. It was far more compact, efficient and effective than those built in Europe at that time.

Using his equipment, Jagadish Chandra Bose demonstrated various important properties of radio waves like reflection and refraction. He made the important discovery that the speed of radio waves was equal to the speed of light— approximately 3×10^5 kilometres per second. Moreover, his equipment generated a new type of radio wave—as small as 1 centimetre to 5 millimetres, now known as 'microwaves'. His equipment proved to be the world's first wireless remote control device. He also invented the world's first 'horn antenna', a conical-shaped antenna to catch microwaves, now commonly used in all microwave-related devices. He successfully demonstrated his experiments before the Lieutenant Governor of Calcutta, Sir William Mackenzie. It established Bose as one of the important successors of the German physicist Heinrich Hertz in India. It has also established Bose as one of the pioneers of wireless telegraphy.

It is believed that Guglielmo Marconi, who is acclaimed as the inventor of the radio, built his radio equipment borrowing ideas from Bose's work.

Bose's findings on radio waves were published in England. The University of London bestowed upon him the Doctor of Science (DSc) degree in 1896. The eminent scientist, Lord Kelvin, congratulated him for his 'wonderful experiments'. Dr Bose had conducted all these experiments without any guidance in research and in the absence of proper laboratory facilities. He had an opportunity to address the meeting of the British Association for the Advancement of Science at Liverpool, England. This lecture-cum-demonstration was attended by eminent British scientists, and it left an indelible mark on modern science, till then considered the hunting ground of only Western scientists.

Now, to be the first and foremost scientist of modern India posed a great challenge to Dr Bose. He waited for an opportunity to prove to the Western world that Indians too can make original contribution to science. Following the footsteps of Michael Faraday and Humphrey Davy, he gave Friday Evening discourse at the prestigious Royal Institution in London where more than five hundred scientists, including luminaries like Oliver Lodge, J.J. Thomson and Lord Kelvin were present. His lecture was hailed and considered valuable for publication in the prestigious scientific journal, *Transactions of the Royal Institution*. He was also invited by other scientific bodies to deliver lectures. Back home, his countrymen greeted Dr Bose. Nobel Laureate Rabindranath Tagore was overjoyed and composed a poem in Bengali where he called Dr Bose, *Vijnan Laksmir Priya* (Beloved of Fairy Science) and presented it to him as a blessing on his return to Calcutta in 1897.

Dr Bose now continued his research in the same small laboratory at the Presidency College. He modified the radio receiver so that it could catch not only radio waves but also visible and invisible light rays. He designed the whole equipment in the form of an eye and even called it an 'Electric eye'. He selected a novel material called 'galena', a compound of metal lead. It has laid the foundation of the subject of 'optical communication' which uses light waves to exchange messages.

One day, while ascertaining the electrical conductivity of his radio receiver, Dr Bose observed a peculiar phenomenon. The receiver behaved normally when used intermittently. But when he used it continuously, its response became slow. Dr Bose was fascinated by this phenomenon which he called 'metal fatigue'. He, therefore, began to study this peculiar response in more detail. For this purpose, he used the highly sensitive current-detecting instrument called 'galvanometer'. He designed a number of experiments and treated several metals and found that their behaviour changed with treatment. He shifted his experiments to plants and found that they were responding more favourably. He had hit upon the underlying unity in the natural world between the inorganic (metals) and the organic, i.e. plants.

Between 1885 and 1901, Dr Bose published a series of papers in prestigious international journals on the production, transmission, properties and applications of millimetre waves, which was the beginning of radio science. His originality and innovation at the dawn of radio science was, in the words of Nobel Laureate Neville Mott, at least 60 years ahead of his time. In fact, it appears that he anticipated the existence of 'p-type' and 'n-type' semiconductors and also developments in such fields as microwave antenna design, application of semiconductor crystals and microwave optics. However, the situation soon changed. He moved on to plant science. Sir Oliver Lodge, the British physicist, started concentrating on parapsychology. Heinrich Hertz, who confirmed the existence of electromagnetic waves, died in 1894. For years, this promising area lay dormant. At the same time, the dramatic success of Guglielmo Marconi in achieving trans-Atlantic propagation in the longer wavelengths created a new communication pathway that holds scientific and commercial attention even today. The course of progress in radio science would have taken a different path had Bose or Lodge continued to do research in the area.

Dr Bose was offered a research-cum-teaching job at a prestigious British university. But he declined the proposal. Again, though he received an offer to patent his findings, he was not after money and declined the offer. The call of his motherland was too strong for him. He returned home with a strong commitment to prove that his theory would work in the Indian environment. He travelled to Europe, the US and Japan, and his findings caught the attention of scientists everywhere. He now devoted himself to a systematic study of plants. He invented several new and highly sensitive instruments, including the 'Crescograph', to measure electrical pulse in plants. He showed that all plants behaved like human beings. They have nerves through which they can sense pleasure and pain. When they are wounded or treated with heat, cold or electric shock, they take considerable time to recover and their reaction time changes. They die when they are poisoned. He also measured the rate of growth of plants during various stages of their life and tried to ascertain the reasons behind their behaviour on the basis of his electrical studies. His findings subsequently influenced subjects like physiology, medicine and agriculture.

Dr Bose presented a very important paper at the International Congress of Physics held in Paris in 1900 titled 'On the Similarity of Responses in Inorganic and Living

Matter'. To prove his point he had devised instruments such as the Crescograph to measure the rate of growth of a plant and the 'death recorder' to record the exact moment of death of a plant. Thus, from a study of electromagnetic waves, especially its property and practical application, Bose turned increasingly to the study of plant and what later came to be known as biophysics. He compared the response of metals, plants and animals to electrical, chemical and mechanical stimulations, and documented them in his famous book, *Responses in the Living and Non-living*, published in 1902. It was his paper rather than his book on radio waves that made him an instant celebrity in the world of science. A leading French newspaper of that time wrote humorously: 'After this discovery we begin to have misgivings when we strike a woman with a blossom, which of them suffers more— the woman or the flower!'

He was conferred the Knighthood in 1916 and was elected a Fellow of the Royal Society of Science (FRS), England, in 1920. His important publications include *Plant Response as a Means of Physiological Investigations, Physiology of Photosynthesis, Nervous Mechanism of Plants* and *Motor Mechanisms of Plants.*

In the early 1900s, Dr Bose realised the need for a good laboratory with proper infrastructure and equipment for Indian scientists to conduct research freely and without disturbance. After retiring from Presidency College in 1915, he invested Rs 400,000 in land and infrastructure of the Institute which was named Bose Institute (*Basu Bigyan Mandir*). A substantial amount of the money was raised as generous public donations. The government pitched in with grants for equipment and laboratories. Rabindranath Tagore, a close friend of Dr Bose, introduced him to several Indian princes, who made generous donations. The Institute started functioning on 30 November 1917. Bose carried on with his research work there until his death in 1937. At present, the Bose Institute is not just a leading research institute; it is equally recognised as an important centre for training PhD students and postdoctoral fellows.

Like Sir J.C. Bose, the Institute's areas of interest are wide and varied. Sir Bose took care to ensure that its scope was not confined to any one area of science but covered all its cognate branches. He said, 'The advancement of science is the principal object of the Institute, and also the diffusion of knowledge.' The emphasis is on finding solutions to problems in agriculture, industry and medicine. True to the ideals of its founder, the Institute tries to address the needs of the nation by fostering quality research on the one hand and turning out highly skilled research personnel on the other. Human resource development has always been one of its main strengths, and, over the years, it has produced scientists working both for the nation and for the advancement of science.

Sir Jagadish Chandra Bose was not just a scholar, scientist and inventor. He was also an ardent nationalist. One can judge his patriotism, courage, integrity and self-respect from the fact that for three years after joining government service in Presidency College, he refused to accept any salary from the British government, since the latter discriminated in the matter of pay scales between British and Indian professors. Finally, the colonial authorities had to give in and allow him the full salary from the day he joined the college. He realised that the best way to fight injustice was to confront it head on.

Sir Bose's versatile genius found expression in literary works also. His *Abyakta* (The Unexpressed) is regarded by literary critics as a masterly exposition of the beauty of natural phenomena. In recognition of his literary works, he was made the President of the Bangiya Sahitya Parishad, the apex body of the state-level literary council for Bengali language and literature. He was also a close friend of Rabindranath Tagore, Swami Vivekananda, Sister Nivedita, and Mahatma Gandhi. Among the eminent scholars abroad, he won the admiration of George Bernard Shaw, Aldous Huxley and Romain Rolland. What all these savants appreciated most was Sir Bose's attempt to prove the age-old humanist faith in the basic unity of life. A British editor once wrote: 'In Sir Jagdish Chandra Bose the culture of 30 centuries has blossomed into a scientific brain of an order which we cannot duplicate in the West.'

Mokshagundam Visvesvaraya

'*I* entertain great regard for your fine abilities and love of the country and that shall be unabated whether I have the good fortune to secure your cooperation or face your honest opposition.' These words are incorporated in a letter addressed to Mokshagundam Visvesvaraya by Mahatma Gandhi. Gandhi and Visvesvaraya played a vital role in their unique ways in shaping the destiny of India. But the means and methods they followed, however, were not always similar; they appeared to be diametrically opposed in certain respects. While Gandhi personified himself as 'Daridranarayana', the god of the poor and was dressed as a *faqir*, Visvesvaraya was always immaculately dressed. And unlike Gandhi, Visvesvaraya was in favour of large-scale industrialisation. Visvesvaraya came to prominence as the architect of big dams and successfully undertook a number of reforms as the *Dewan* of Mysore; Gandhi attained universal fame by showing the world that one can achieve his goals by following the path of truth and non-violence.

Mokshagundam Visvesvaraya was born on 28 August 1860 in a village known as Muddenahalli, in Chikballapur

Taluk, Kolur district, Mysore State (now Karnataka). His father was Srinivasa Sastry and mother Venkatalakshammu. Mokshagundam is an *Agrahara*, a place where Brahmins live, in the village of Siddarpur in the Kurnool district of Andhra Pradesh. It is a centre of pilgrimage. Hindus believe that a dip in the small tank of this village will wash away one's sins. Visvesvaraya's ancestors lived in this village, gifted to them by a local chieftain. Hence Mokshagundam became a permanent abode of the family and its descendants.

Visvesvaraya lost his father when he was only fifteen. He completed his lower secondary studies at Chikballapur, but his widowed mother did not have sufficient money to finance his higher studies. Her brother H. Ramaiah, who stayed in Bangalore, took Visvesvaraya under his care. The boy was taken to Bangalore where he was admitted to Wesleyan Mission High School in 1875. After completing his high school education, Visvesvaraya joined Central College. He started teaching privately to finance his education. He used to walk with his books to the Bungalow of Muddiah in the fort area. Muddiah was one of the ministers of the Maharaja of Mysore. Visvesvaraya was a private tutor to the minister's sons. Finishing his tuition, he would walk back to Ramaiah's residence in Chamarajapet, a distance of one mile. After having his meal he would rush to Central College at a distance of not less than three miles. In this way, Visvesvaraya would walk not less than ten miles a day.

Visvesvaraya stood first in engineering and in 1884 joined the engineer's cadre. Bombay was then a very big province. It consisted of Gujarat, Maharashtra and parts of Karnataka. He was placed in charge of Nasik district, and was entrusted with the construction of a siphon on the river Panjra at Dashari, a village thirty-five miles from Dhulia. From the river Panjra, water had to be transported through a hill to the other side by siphon. Rocks had to be drilled to pass the water through a tunnel. Pipes had to be fitted for the free flow of water. He started the work with confidence. But soon monsoon rains started pouring. The river became swollen. He found that continuing work under such circumstances would entail wasteful expenditure exceeding the grant. He wrote to the District Executive Engineer seeking permission to suspend the work and return to Dhulia, his headquarters. The reply he received was disappointing: to suspend the work would amount to disobedience. Visvesvaraya decided to accept the challenge and complete the work as directed. He used to go to the work site riding a horse, covering two-and-a-half miles across the river. One day, it rained so heavily that he could not return to his camp as the river was in spate and swollen. He had to remain at the work site till the floods subsided. Later, he swam across the river to his camp with the help of rafts built by the Bhils. His horse was transported by the labour.

Visvesvaraya completed the work within the stipulated time of two months. The water flowed through freely and the construction was completed satisfactorily. The Executive Engineer, who happened to be an Englishman, expressed appreciation of the work and took back the adverse remarks that he had previously made. Visvesvaraya was now keen to work in a higher rank. The Executive Engineer encouraged him to appear for the necessary examination. He learned Marathi, essential for the examination, and emerged successful. Within twenty months of his entering the service he reached the first grade. Though born in Karnataka, he became proficient in Marathi. He was posted to Khandesh but unfortunately got affected with malaria. He requested for transfer, and from Irrigation he was placed in charge of the Roads and Buildings division in Poona (Pune).

Visvesvaraya was posted to Sakkur in Sind, which was then a part of Bombay Presidency. His job was to provide drinking water to Sakkur from the river Sindhu. Here he was expected to be his own master. As per the plan already prepared and sanctioned, water had to be pumped from the river to the nearby hill, filtered and supplied through pipes. The Municipality was not in a position to fund the erection of the filters. Visvesvaraya's ingenuity worked. He got a circular well dug in the river bed and connected it with a tunnel dug under the river. The water percolating through the sand to the bottom of the well was filtered and purified. This water was then pumped up to the tank on the hill. The turbid water of the river thus purified was supplied to the city through pipes. The Municipality was spared the expenses.

On another occasion, Poona and the nearby military station of Karkee were being provided with water from a canal of the river Musa. The canal water flowed to the lake Fife. It was stored there. Karkee got filtered water and Poona unfiltered water. The stored water was not sufficient for the growing city. In summer, the lake would dry up and in the rainy season it would overflow. One way was to raise the height of the waste weir. This would result in heavy expenditure and the raised wall might not be strong enough to bear the weight and pressure of the escaping water. This spelt danger to the towns below. The problem had to be faced and solved. Visvesvaraya used his intelligence. He designed automatic gates by which the storage capacity of the lake would be increased. He got these automatic gates installed on the surplus weir of Fife. The gates could hold up water in the lake up to eight feet above the waste weir. To hold more would endanger the safety of the dam. But when the water rose above eight feet, the gates automatically opened allowing surplus water to escape. When the level of water fell below eight feet they automatically closed.

In 1899, Visvesvaraya was transferred to Poona from Surat. There he found that an adequate supply of water to all the cultivators was a problem. The upper regions under the Musa canal got copious supply of water, but lower down it was not sufficient for irrigation. The *ryots* were displeased. He devised a new system to ensure sufficient water by rotation. He summoned a conference of *zamindars*, *ryots* and concerned officials. He explained to them the 'Block System' which envisaged the same amount of water being used for irrigating a larger area by triennial rotation of crops which would also facilitate improvement in the fertility of land with no water wastage. The Government of India appointed a top-level Power Commission to suggest suitable steps to increase cultivation of crops by irrigation. Visvesvaraya submitted a comprehensive memorandum expounding the Block System of irrigation. He was cross-examined by the Commission for three days and his plan was recommended for adoption.

Visvesvaraya rose quickly in official esteem and cadre. In 1904, he became the Sanitary Engineer to the Bombay Government. In 1907, he was in charge of three different divisions as Chief Engineer. He was appointed a member of the committee to revise the scheme of engineering studies. He prepared and submitted schemes for providing water to Poona, Dharwar and Bijapur. In 1906, he was entrusted with the responsibility to suggest ways and means to solve the water problem in Aden. There he surveyed the area, and collected facts and figures from reports. The area around Aden, for a distance of sixty miles, was mountainous. Rain was scarce. Rainwater would flow down as a little stream and disappear in sandy Lahex, eighteen miles from Aden. He recommended the digging of a well there, pump the water to a storage tank on a nearby hill and supply the water to Aden through conduit pipes. He carried out a detailed survey of the area to lay underground pipes. In recognition of his valuable services Visvesvaraya was awarded the Kaiser-I-Hind.

Kolhapur is famous for its temple dedicated to Mahalakshmi. The state was governed by a Hindu ruler. The big tank here was made of mud. It was the source of drinking water to the city. Once, a large portion of the tank bund breached causing danger to the tank itself. The water in the tank was likely to leak out resulting in a shortage of drinking water to the city. Visvesvaraya immediately rushed to Kolhapur. He closely examined the condition of the tank, and prepared a plan for the repair of the bund and restoration of the tank. He visited Kolhapur three or four times to see how the repair work was being carried out and completed at the earliest. The bund became stronger and more stable than before. There was heavy rain, but the bund did not give way.

Even though Visvesvaraya was getting promoted rapidly, there was no chance of his being elevated to the post of Chief Engineer. He, therefore, resigned. He retired from the Bombay Government Service in May 1908. Thereafter, he started on a tour of the Western countries to acquire knowledge. After his sojourn in USA, Canada and Russia, he returned to India in April 1909. On 15 April, he became the Chief Engineer of Hyderabad State. He was to submit projects to protect the city of Hyderabad, facilitate underground sewage for Hyderabad and Bidarghat, and sanitation for Hyderabad city. He secured the services of engineers who were known to him from his Bombay Government Service days. He got the entire area of the river Moosi surveyed and went through official records of the previous floods. He collected data of rainfall in the neighbouring Bombay and Madras provinces. He studied the figures of heavy rainfall in different parts of the world. He found that in the catchment area of the river

Moosi, above Hyderabad, there were 788 small tanks, which worked out at five tanks to every three square miles of catchment area. Of these, 221 tanks gave way owing to the recent floods. He identified the place where the heaviest rainfall had occurred and where the reservoir broke down and when. The water which flowed out had a speed of four miles per hour. He found that smaller the catchment area, greater the effect of the floods. He proposed the construction of one dam across the Moosi at a distance of eighty-two miles above the city, and another across the Easi, a tributary of Moosi, at a distance of six and a half miles. To raise the banks of the river within the city and convert the area on either side into walks and gardens were a few of the important proposals put forward by him. The work was undertaken in 1913 and before the construction was completed, Visvesvaraya had become the *Dewan* of Mysore. But he continued to visit Hyderabad to supervise the construction of the dams and other schemes submitted by him. These dams, known as Himayatsagar and Osmansagar, provide water to the twin cities of Hyderabad and Secunderabad. Today, for the improved drainage, plenty of water and electricity, the credit goes to Visvesvaraya.

In view of Visvesvaraya's extraordinary calibre, the Maharaja of Mysore appointed him as the Chief Engineer. He was also Secretary to the Railways and occupied this important post for three years till he became the *Dewan* of Mysore in November 1912. At this time, two committees were created, one for technical education and another for industrial development in the state. Visvesvaraya was the president of both these committees.

In appreciation of the work done by Visvesvaraya during his tenure as Chief Engineer for three years, the Maharaja appointed him as *Dewan* of Mysore. As an engineer he had to work within certain limits as directed by the state, but now as *Dewan*, he had sufficient freedom to give concrete shape to his ideas. Visvesvaraya attached great importance to the spread of education. After he became *Dewan*, primary education was made compulsory in the state of Mysore. For the first time, special grants were made for the education of the depressed communities and backward classes. Maharani's College in Mysore was raised to a first grade college with the addition of Bachelor of Arts courses in 1917. The first hostel for women students was opened in Mysore in 1917. Special courses in Kannada for the benefit of small farmers, courses for small shopkeepers in elementary account keeping, banking, and commercial geography, shorthand and typing were introduced. An agricultural school was opened in Hebbal near Bangalore in 1913, with a large farm attached to it for practical instruction. Mechanical training institutions were founded in all the district headquarters. Public libraries were opened in Mysore and Bangalore.

Krishnaraja Sagar Dam, in the vicinity of the renowned Brindavan Gardens, is reminiscent of Visvesvaraya's ingenuity. The dam was conceived not only for the purpose of irrigation, it also included a provision for providing electricity to the Kolar goldfields. As the work of construction was proceeding, the river Cauvery rose in spate. Visvesvaraya directed the work to be carried out with greater enthusiasm. He advised 2,000 more labourers to be taken in where 10,000 had already been employed. The gold company had agreed to pay more provided the assured supply was given from July 1915. This was an additional incentive to complete the work in time. He directed the work to be carried on non-stop day and night, advising the use of bright 'Washington' lights during the night. Doctors were appointed to treat workers afflicted by malaria. He directed the Chief Engineer, the Inspector General of

Police and the Deputy Commissioner of the district to camp at the spot to speed up the work, to look after the security of the persons and property, and supervise the work in general. When the Mysore Representative Assembly was in session he used to preside over its deliberations from 11 am to 5 pm and immediately afterwards proceeded by car to the dam site. His presence redoubled the efforts of officers and men to work with renewed energy. He had arranged to get reports on the progress of the work every half hour by telephone. Facing with courage all unexpected problems and difficulties, he got the work completed well in time. Power was also supplied to Kolar goldfields by July 1915.

Visvesvaraya drew up plans to improve the condition of the villages. Village and agricultural committees were formed. He divided village activities under six broad heads: agriculture, subsidiary occupations, education, industries, manufacture and trade, and village communal work including settlement of disputes and village administration. All these were gradually entrusted to village *panchayats* which later came into existence. Every *panchayat* was at liberty to draw up its own plan for progress. He encouraged them to be self-reliant rather than be dependent on the government for everything. A Department of Agriculture was formed. Apple orchards and coconut, coffee and fruit plantations received special impetus. The village *panchayats* were entrusted with the distribution of water on a fair basis.

The Maharaja of Mysore entrusted Visvesvaraya with the responsibility of Mysore Iron & Steel Works, making him its Chairman. Visvesvaraya constituted a new Board of Management. Different sections were brought under one unified control. He detailed the work to be handled by each department and made the heads of sections responsible for the execution of work entrusted to each one of them. He dispensed with the services of all the American experts and appointed Indian engineers and chemists in the vacancies thus created. He generated patriotic fervour among them by his own example and encouraged young men to acquire practical experience and shoulder greater responsibilities. He sent some young recruits to foreign countries and to Jamshedpur to work as apprentices and acquire practical experience. He himself toured Sweden, England, USA and Germany at his own cost to gain firsthand knowledge of manufacturing iron by wood charcoal. By closely studying the process, he was able to solve some of the problems which his own organisation was facing. The works which were running at a loss now turned a new leaf and began to earn profit. He did not accept any honorarium for his work at the Works. In September 1929, Visvesvaraya retired from the office of the Chairman of Mysore Iron & Steel Works.

Visvesvaraya can be credited with economic planning in India. As early as in 1911, even before he became *Dewan* of Mysore, he drew up five-year plans. He held the first economic conference in Mysore in 1911 and suggested that intellectuals and social scientists should draw up plans with the cooperation of both the rulers and the ruled. The publication of *Reconstructing India* in 1920 by Sir Visvesvaraya from London was the first attempt to make the people of India plan-conscious. He started agricultural and horticultural shows and established agricultural schools and experimental farms. Rehabilitation of the handloom industry was also taken up. A Central Government weaving factory was established to provide weavers with latest designs and techniques in weaving. The State Bank of Mysore was founded in 1913 for financing the projects.

Prior to 1916, sandalwood was being auctioned in Mysore and the purchasers used to export it to France, Italy, and

Germany where it was treated to yield sandal oil, the base for various perfumes and toiletries. The oil used to be re-exported to India for consumption in this country. Visvesvaraya wanted to stop this commercial exploitation. He requested the Indian Institute of Science to conduct research and they succeeded in extracting oil from sandalwood. This eventually led to the establishment of the Sandal Oil Factory in Mysore in 1916. It became an ingredient for the sandal soap. A soap factory was also established. Various institutes were also started to expand the range of utility products from sandal oil. Rice mills, oil mills, sugarcane crushing mills and power looms sprang up everywhere. Thus industrialisation in the state picked up momentum. It was Visvesvaraya who gave the clarion call, 'Industrialise or Perish'.

Soon after he became *Dewan* of Mysore, various efforts were made for the amelioration of the backward classes and untouchables. Equal opportunity was created for them to get themselves educated. He founded Century Club in Bangalore and was also the founder of Deccan Club in Poona. He advised people not to succumb to the feeling that 'fate' is conspiring against us, and to give up the thought that we are being tossed about helplessly in this *Samsara Sagara* (world ocean) by the invincible, inexorable Law of *Karma* (fate) which has ordained our present and future. Visvesvaraya was a strong opponent of superstitious beliefs and practices. He founded the Civic and Social Progress Association. Scholarships were granted to students of backward communities. Widow marriage was encouraged. Child marriage was strongly discouraged. Education was free for women. Separate schools were opened for Muslims and for those who wanted to learn Urdu. But he did not give room for separatism to grow. He discouraged separatist tendencies. He encouraged social parties and common dining to break caste barrier and customs. Steps were taken to enlarge the scope, powers and functions of local self-governing institutions in the state, to increase their financial resources and make them real, responsible and effective agents in the administration of their local affairs. He introduced a system of Efficiency Audit with a view to ensuring continuous action required for maintaining discipline and efficiency in government departments and service personnel. Thus, over time, Mysore came to be seen as a model state.

After India achieved independence, the then Prime Minister Jawaharlal Nehru sought Visvesvaraya's assistance in laying a bridge across the Ganges. Visvesvaraya was ninety years old then. He did an aerial reconnaissance of the Ganges from Jangipur up to twenty miles upstream of Patna by a chartered plane flying at a low altitude. During the flight, he sat in the co-pilot's seat in order to have a better view of the course of the river. From Calcutta to Kathmandu he and his associates travelled by rail, steamer and motorcar inspecting every possible spot. Discussions were held with the concerned technical officers, representatives of Trade and Commerce and other public bodies. At Delhi, he had discussions with the Chief of Army Staff General Thimayya and Quartermaster-General Thorat, to ascertain their opinions on the location of the site from the strategic point of view. He personally prepared a format and decided the number of chapters and contents of each chapter. After examining the large volume of data in full detail, he recommended that the site at Mokameh was most suitable for the purpose. The construction work was started in September 1953 and completed in March 1959, and the bridge was opened on 1 May 1959.

All this brought Visvesvaraya eternal fame. The universities of Calcutta, Patna, Allahabad, Jadavpur, Bombay, Varanasi,

Andhra and Mysore conferred on him *Honoris Causa*. The President of India honoured him with the highest distinction of Bharat Ratna. The birth centenary of Visvesvaraya was celebrated all over India and abroad on 15 September 1960. Prime Minister Jawaharlal Nehru paid his personal tributes to him as dreamer, thinker and man of action not lost in the past but always thinking of the future, living an integrated life, and bringing into existence and giving shape to dreams not for himself but for India and her people.

After Visvesvaraya crossed the age of hundred his poor health confined him to bed. His sight was good but his hearing became weak. Yet he was still interested in the economic development of the country. He sent a message to the Prime Minister to make birth control compulsory as in Japan. Such was his concern for the future of the country. A grand old man and the giant among engineers passed away on 12 April 1962 at the age of 102 years. He had prepared his last testament and will, and in accordance with his last wishes, his mortal remains were taken to Muddenahalli, his birthplace, and cremated there with official honours.

'Success in life depends on action, that is, on what you do, and not what you feel or think and the price of success is hard work.' This was, in fact, exemplified by Visvesvaraya during his lifetime. He was by birth poor, by tradition a gentleman, by occupation an engineer, by circumstances a *Dewan*, mentally a scientist, and by efforts an industrialist. He had the courage of conviction and strength of mind to act accordingly. He had been a combination of endeavour, adventure, courage, intellect, capacity and strength.

Chandrasekhar Venkata Raman

The 'Raman Effect' has opened new vistas to our knowledge of the structure of matter. The inventor of the Raman Effect in light scattering, C.V. Raman, contributed extensively to the realm of light and wave by monitoring the light waves passing through molecules of different elements. He explained the phenomenon by comparing it with a person throwing a tennis ball at a certain speed at a tennis player who is waving his bat back and forth. If the bat is moving backward when the ball hits the bat, the ball will lose some of its speed and bounce back with a reduced speed. Again, when the ball hits the bat while the latter is moving forward, the ball will gain speed from the forward motion of the bat and bounce back at a greater speed. This epoch-making discovery brought the propounder of Raman Effect, C.V. Raman, at par with scientists of the first rung the world over.

What motivated Raman to achieve the extraordinary against all odds? What was the secret behind his success? His life provides a glimpse of the basis of his success in life. He blossomed at a time when the British held sway over India, and when only a small number of individuals took to science and went to Europe for higher studies and research. By the dawn of the twentieth century there were only a few Indian scientists and one or two scientific societies in Bengal. The names of Acharya Jagadish Chandra Bose, the physicist-cum-botanist, and Prafulla Chandra Ray, the chemist, were well known. But laboratories in India were ill-equipped and there were only a handful of fledgling scientific institutions. However, the pioneers gave a valuable start. Chandrasekhar Venkata Raman, who rose to the pinnacle of science in India, was one such person.

Raman was the second child of a local schoolteacher. Chandrasekhar Iyer lived in the small village of Thiruvanaikkavall near Thiruchirapalli in south India. He was born on 7 November 1888. His mother was Parvathi Ammal. His parents had eight children: five sons and three daughters. His brother, Subramanya Ayyar, was an expert musicologist who mastered the violin at his father's inspiration. When Raman was just four years old, his father accepted lectureship in mathematics and physics in the coastal town of Vishakhapatnam. In spite of a large family and small salary (Rs 85 per month), Chandrasekhar Iyer had a good collection of books on physics, mathematics and philosophy.

Since his childhood days, Raman was keen on learning science. While he was in middle school, he used to go through books on science meant for levels far in advance of his age. He performed experiments with improvised apparatus at home and in school. He matriculated at the age of eleven, and joined Presidency College on a scholarship. When he was just fifteen, he passed Bachelor of Arts in the first class winning gold medals in English and physics. He obtained his Master's degree in January 1907.

There is a photograph of Raman taken while he was in the Presidency College—a thin unimpressive boy with a *dhoti* draped around him, with a cap and no *chappal* on his feet.

There is a story that one of the professors at the college could not believe that this inconspicuous lad was a student of the Presidency College. He asked Raman whether he had come there by mistake. It caused general laughter in the classroom. Very soon, his professors exempted him from attending all the science classes as they felt he had nothing to learn from them.

At the age of sixteen, while measuring the angle of a prism using a college spectrometer, Raman observed some diffraction bands. He started investigating and the research formed the subject of his first publication in *The Philosophical Magazine* (London). This was followed by a note in the same journal on a new experimental method of measuring surface tension. In college, he spent much of his time in the library studying Lord Raleigh's scientific papers. He bicycled twice a week to the Connemara Library, several miles away, to read the latest scientific journals. He learnt from Helmholtz's *Sensations of Tone* what research really means, and ventured boldly into experimental research in the college laboratory, which had no previous tradition of research in physics. He corresponded with Lord Raleigh who was then the President of the Royal Society.

When Raman passed his Bachelor's examination, his teachers suggested that he should go to England for further studies. But the Civil Surgeon of Madras (now, Chennai) ruled it out by disqualifying him medically, saying that the rigours of the English climate would 'kill' him. In 1906, his teachers advised him to appear for the competitive examination which chose civil servants for the finance department. He passed the examination topping the list.

Raman married Lokasundari. What attracted him when he saw her for the first time was her expertise on the *veena*. She was playing the famous Thyagaraja composition, *'Rama ni samanam evaro'* meaning 'Who is equal to you, Rama?'

on the musical instrument. Lokasundari must have hit the right chords not only on the *veena* but in Raman's heart. He firmly resolved to take her as his partner after the meeting. In his quest for scientific knowledge, Lokasundari stood by Raman devotedly throughout her life. She once related with a smile how difficult it was to turn Raman's attention from scientific pursuits to the obligations of matrimony.

In 1917, Raman accepted the offer of Sir Tarakanath Palit Professorship of Physics at the University College of Science, Calcutta (now Kolkata), even though it meant giving up a lucrative job in exchange for one with five times less emoluments. This, however, provided him an opportunity to enter the Indian Association for the Cultivation of Science at any time of the day or night. He had complete access to the laboratories of the Association to carry out his experiments. Often, he worked till very late at night but still appeared in time on the following day for lecture at the University College of Science.

Raman's first trip abroad was to England in 1921 to attend the Congress of Universities of the British Empire at Oxford. He represented the University of Calcutta at the Congress. It provided him an opportunity to meet some of the leading scientists of the day. His lecture at the Physical Society of London on his latest researches in optics and acoustics with experimental demonstrations drew the attention of a large number of physicists.

During his return voyage, Raman became fascinated with the deep blue colour of the sea. Sometime back, Lord Raleigh had explained that the blue colour of the sky was due to the scattering of sunlight by the molecules constituting the atmosphere. Raman's marvellous intuition led him to examine the colour of the ocean very critically during his voyage using nicol prism. Immediately after arriving in Calcutta, Raman started critical laboratory experiments with samples of water kept in clean rectangular glass vessels and illuminated laterally with a strong parallel beam of light. He observed the track of the beam in a perpendicular direction. During the course of a month he carried out several crucial experiments with water. The disturbing effect of dust was eliminated by using distilled water kept at rest for many weeks. The lateral scattering now came but as a feeble blue track that was highly polarised. The intensity of scattering by water, as observed and calculated from the Einstein-Smolouchowski formula, was shown to be just 160 times stronger than in pure dust-free air.

Raman wrote his classical paper on 'The Molecular Scattering of Light in Water and the Colour of the Sea' within a month of his return to India. It was published in the *Proceedings of the Royal Society of London* (Vol A.101, pp 64-80). Immediately thereafter in 1922, he wrote his memoir *The Molecular Diffraction of Light*. In this, he outlined plans for further experimental researches to be undertaken urgently to investigate the molecular diffraction of light by matter in the gaseous, liquid and solid states during its transition from the gaseous to the liquid and from the liquid to the solid states, in liquid mixtures, in solutions and in relation to chemical constitution. He also discussed the possible implications of the quantum theory.

In 1924, Raman's outstanding researches won him worldwide recognition and the Royal Society of London conferred on him the high distinction of Fellow of the Royal Society (FRS) at the young age of thirty-six. In June 1924, he was invited by the British Association of Science to inaugurate discussion on 'The Scattering of Light' at its session in Toronto. He also attended the International Congress of Mathematicians as a representative of the University of Calcutta during the centenary of the famous Franklin Institute in Philadelphia, USA. There he met the leading American physicist, R.A. Millikan, who invited him to the California Institute of Technology. There he delivered a regular course of lectures on thermodynamics to a group of American physicists and senior scholars at the Norman Bridge Laboratory of Physics.

Raman involved his research scholars in the study of the scattering of light in water and 65 different carefully purified liquids. He derived a formula for Compton scattering using the classical theory. This helped him realise that 'weak fluorescence' might be the incoherent scattering with a change of wavelength, analogous to the Compton scattered radiation. It was found that in pure glycerine the scattered light was greenish in colour instead of the usual blue, and that radiation was strongly polarised. This gave him fresh impetus to take up the problem. The presence of 'weak fluorescence' was observed by Raman in a number of organic liquids and vapours. Nearly 80 different aromatic, aliphatic and inorganic liquids were examined and the effect was seen in all cases, including the universal characters of the phenomenon. His team detected the new radiation in vapours of ether and amylene. This new phenomenon was published in *Nature*, a weekly scientific journal published from the UK, in its March 1928 issue.

The apparatus used by Raman for his discovery consisted of a mirror for deflecting sunlight, condensing lens of complementary glass filers, a flask containing benzene, and a pocket spectroscope. The discovery was the culmination of seven years of systematic and sustained work carried out with devotion by Raman and his band of students. When in October 1928, Arnold Sommerfield visited Raman's laboratory, he was impressed with his work as a world-class scientist on the verge of discovering the light-scattering effect. He proposed Raman as a candidate for the Nobel Prize to the Committee. Raman received the Prize in 1930 at the age of forty-two, which in a way also endorsed the high levels of scientific research in India.

In 1933, Raman was appointed Director of the Indian Institute of Science. For him, it was a welcome change after being in Calcutta for twenty-five years, both from the view of the climate and the beautiful environment. He was the first Indian Director of the Institute. He felt that research and advanced education could be the foundations for economic advancement only if there was excellence of the highest order. Therefore, he tried many strategies to bring about change at the Indian Institute of Science. He sought to improve the surroundings by planting beautiful flowering trees. A number of Indian scientists leaving India were offered permanent and lucrative positions. The Department of Physics in the Institute was developed with characteristic energy. He started research in diverse fields, viz. ultrasonics, Brillouin scattering, X-ray scattering, physics of the diamond and lattice dynamics. Light scattering studies continued as a regular programme in his laboratory. One of his outstanding contributions during his fifteen-year tenure at the Institute concerned the diffraction of light by high frequency sound waves. He himself published several papers. Though his outlook was essentially that of an experimental physicist, he would insist on the physical significance of every theoretical result.

It was in the field of lattice dynamics that Raman got involved in a bitter controversy with Born, Debye and others by strongly opposing their theories. He had a lively and life-long interest in diamonds and built up an outstanding collection. He made many scientific studies on the diamond, but recognition came to him for his fine contribution in optics, spectroscopy and crystal physics. He was, in fact, the moving spirit behind the tremendous work at the Institute.

Raman had visions of a private institute in which he could continue his scientific research after he retired from the Indian Institute of Science. The Maharajah of Mysore gifted him 11 acres of land in a prime locality in Bangalore for this purpose. He arranged to build his institute on this land in 1948 when he retired. It is known as Raman Research Institute. There he applied the criteria of ability and proven merit rather than paper qualification for the induction of staff. The candidates were also evaluated in their own way. He was always keen to provide ample facilities for research and bought several microscopes and electronic equipment that the US military and air force released by DGTD to educational and research institutions from what the American armed forces had left behind after the Second World War. They included magnetrons, microwave generators, oscilloscopes, transmitting equipment, servo-systems, aerial cameras, optical systems, infra-red viewers and detectors. A large number of machine tools and lathes, and a liquid nitrogen plant were also part of his windfall. Radhakrishnan, the youngest son of Raman, was an amateur radio expert and had helped in choosing most of the electronic equipment. He also built some beautiful museums in the Institute.

Raman had a great fascination for diamonds. He had a collection of about 600 diamonds of different kinds and origins. These were from various sources, gifts and purchases. He used them all in his studies, classified them according to their properties and boxed them beautifully. He was decorated by the Maharajah of Mysore with a pendant studded with 63 diamonds. The beautiful piece of jewellery promptly entered the scientific literature as Raman studied the diamonds set in pendant and drew several interesting conclusions about the nature and intensity of luminescence exhibited by diamonds when excited by ultra-violet light. As a result, a series of articles were published on the subject in *Proceedings of the Indian Academy of Sciences.*

Raman gradually became interested in the physiology of vision. He educated himself thoroughly on the anatomy and physiology of the eye and how it functioned as the visual apparatus par excellence. He carried out simple experiments with colour filters, using himself and others as guinea pigs. The culmination of this work was the publication of the treatise *The Physiology of Vision.*

The origin of colour in beetles and butterflies interested Raman and he wrote a paper on the subject demonstrating that a regular periodic structure in their wings produced the beautiful colours due to the diffraction of light. The colour, a brilliant metallic blue or bluish green, depended on the angle of observation. As he was fascinated with colours due to pigments in butterflies and with a view to enlarge his collection, he used to go to his country estate in Kengeri with a net bag attached to a long pole. At the age of sixty-five, running after the butterflies as they flitted from one branch to another, he carried out this operation with great enthusiasm for several weeks. The specimens were put in a jar and brought to the Institute where they were mounted in glass cases.

Raman maintained his health remarkably well until a few months before his death. His daily walks, dietary habits, and means of relaxation helped him keep good health. At sixty-one, he developed hernia but in 1952 this took a serious turn. He had to undergo surgery at the Vellore American Mission Hospital. It was extremely difficult for the doctor to keep him in bed. Doctor Sommerfield had to admonish him saying if he did not follow his instructions, he would not be able to do anything.

Raman bequeathed all his personal wealth to his Institute. He was very much against accepting grants from the government as he apprehended that this would destroy the freedom necessary for carrying out fundamental research. When M.C. Chagla, the then Education Minister of India, offered government support, Raman said, 'Sir, I want this Institute to be an oasis in the desert, free from government interference.' He regarded the Institute as a place for his work during his lifetime and, after that, as a legacy to the succeeding generations of scientists in India. On his retirement from the Indian Institute of Science at the age of sixty, the Indian government appointed him a National Professor for life to enable him to pursue his interest at the new Institute.

Even at seventy-eight, Raman kept himself as active as an eighteen-year-old. He had a tremendous sense of humour. Replying to the speeches made at a meeting organised by Vikram Sarabhai to celebrate Raman's eightieth birthday, he said, 'You know, people may be wondering why I wear turban in this day and age. I will tell you why. The turban is a bandage to prevent my getting the swollen head after hearing such speeches. . . .' He lamented that there was so much to be studied and understood that he felt he had not accomplished anything worthwhile in his life.

Less than a couple of months before his death, on 2 October 1970, Raman went up to the first floor of the Raman Research Institute, seemingly as active as a young schoolboy, and delivered the Gandhi Memorial Lecture. It was the last lecture he delivered, a masterly exposition of his ideas about the theory of hearing, once again illustrating his breadth of interests. This incident also illustrates that he not only believed in work but also practised what he believed in, by keeping himself active till the very end. He suffered heart attack and passed away on 21 November 1970. According to his wishes, his mortal remains were cremated in the grounds of the Raman Research Institute.

Raman took keen interest in geology. His knowledge of rocks and rock-forming minerals would surprise even a seasoned geologist. He had, in his museum, a lovely collection of different types of granites, all polished to expose their structure, colour and constituent minerals. Likewise, he had specimens of limestone from all over the world. He also took keen interest in meteorology. At the age of eighty, he wrote two scientific papers about the origin of jet streams and the general circulation of the atmosphere. All the best roses that the Bangalore nurseries could supply were planted in his rose garden under his supervision and he admired them like a child. He never missed the annual horticultural shows in the Lal Bagh gardens located near the south Kempegowda tower in Bangalore. When the crowd had melted away, he was still there standing amidst the flowers with a magnifying glass in one hand and a beautiful begonia in the other. He was seen studying the colour patterns through the glass.

Raman was typically Indian. He never gave up his old traditional hairdo. In public, he always sported a turban. 'How else,' he quipped, 'could Lord Rutherford have recognised me in that crowded Cavendish lecture hall?' He despised all kinds of rituals. On the night he died, his wife asked him to take the name of God. He replied, 'I believe only in the spirit of man,' and talked of the Buddha, the Christ and the Mahatma, and then made a request, 'Just a clean and simple cremation for me, no mumbo-jumbo please.'

To conclude, Chandrasekhar Venkata Raman was indeed a *karmayogi*. He was neither a religious person nor an atheist. He was, in fact, a self-made man having an indomitable will, with total absorption in science. His dedication to science was so intense and in tune with the traditions of Indian scholarship that it would be justified to describe him as a real *rishi*. Nature was his object of worship, and the mysteries of the universe constituted the goals of his meditation.

Meghnad Saha

'To have a comprehensive idea of the New Age, we should look at the kind of life pursued in a country like USA, England or Germany and the present system of industrial production in these countries and contrast it with the course of human life and industry in the same countries two centuries ago. . . . The task before India is, therefore, to organise her industrial life according to the neo-technical method of production.' These words of Meghnad Saha, which formed his presidential address delivered on the occasion of the foundation stone laying ceremony of the Students Hall of the Institute of Nuclear Physics on 19 January 1956, underlines his vision of a resurgent India. Meghnad Saha had been a brilliant scientist with a vision of an organised scientific community of research institutions to compete with the best in the Western world and of directing the scientific manpower of the country to the task of national reconstruction. Harnessing of our mighty rivers occupied a place of pride in his dream. His was not simply a dream, but a burning passion and zeal.

Meghnad Saha was born in October 1893 in Seoratali, a village 45 kilometres from Dacca, now the capital of

Bangladesh. He was the son of Jagannath Saha, owner of a small grocery shop. His mother was Bhubaneswari. The couple had two sons and two daughters, when a fifth child was born. It was a stormy night when Meghnad was born, amidst the lashing of rain and thunder. A howling wind blew off the thatched roof of the cottage where the newborn lay huddled in his mother's arms. Since the frenzy of Nature showed little sign of abating, the grandmother, in due reverence to the rain-gods, named the baby Meghnad, meaning 'the roll of thunder'. It was altogether a fitting scene for the arrival of someone who, like the son of King Ravana, turned out to be an uncompromising fighter till his last breath. Meghnad was a healthy child and, like most village children, learnt to swim and row quite early.

The river Bansai was on the outskirts of the village. During the monsoon months, the river overflowed its banks flooding the fields and open grounds to a point of inaccessibility. Every house was compelled to have its own boat. As the water gradually receded, it would wash away some of the soil along with it. To prevent soil erosion, people stuck poles or planted trees around their houses. At times, boundary walls, made of galvanised iron sheets, were put up as a protection against the fury of the river.

Meghnad joined the village primary school at the age of seven, where his teachers were struck by his uncanny memory and aptitude for learning. The boy seldom forgot anything he once learnt. He had no other interest apart from his books. His family, however, attached little value to education and his parents were far from happy to see their son turn out to be so studious. They would have preferred to have him assist the father in his shop. It was a common sight to see young Meghnad carry food to the shop, an umbrella over his head and a pile of books under his arm. But Meghnad had no interest in selling groceries. Often, his father would lash at his son with a stick when the son's loud reading disturbed his sleep. But his elder brother Jainath was very keen to see his younger brother have proper education. To finance his education, Meghnad had to attend to minor household chores and tend the cow of Ananta Kumar Das, the person who sponsored Meghnad's education. Every weekend, Meghnad would walk back home. When the village became flooded he would row all the way.

At the age of twelve, Meghnad joined the Collegiate School in Dacca. It was then, for the first time, that the village boy got a glimpse of a world different from his own. After the middle school examination, he again stood first in the Dacca division and was awarded a scholarship of four rupees per month. In addition to this, he regularly received the monthly allowance of five rupees from his brother Jainath. During the summer and *puja* holidays he went home to his village where he helped his father bathe the cattle. Mathematics was his first love in school, while history was a close second. He was exceptionally fond of reading Todd's *Rajasthan*. Tagore's *Katha O Kahini*, which glorifies the valour of the Rajput and Maratha braves, was his favourite book. *Meghnad Badh*, the epic poem of Madhusudan Dutt, delighted him to no end. It was always the fighting spirit which never failed to appeal to him. Above all, a striking feature of his character was his intense passion for and capacity to absorb knowledge. He took to attending Bible classes held by the Dacca Baptist Mission. He obtained top position in the all-Bengal examination of the Baptist Mission which was open to college students as well. In the entrance examination, he stood first among the students of the then East Bengal. He scored the highest marks in mathematics and in the languages. In 1909, he joined Dacca College as a student of Intermediate Science.

Meghnad took private lessons in German from Professor Nagendra Nath Sen who had just returned from Vienna with a doctorate in chemistry. In the Intermediate examination, Meghnad stood third in order of merit. But throughout his life he carried the imprint of his Seoratali boyhood. He had serious concern for the control of flood waters. He never bothered to dress up in style. His mother always encouraged him in his studies. She even pawned one of her gold bangles to pay for his examination fees. To express his gratitude to his mother, Meghnad later set up a girls' school in Seoratali, naming it Bhubaneswari after his mother.

In 1911, Meghnad joined the Presidency College for his graduation in science. In 1913, his chemistry teacher, P.C. Ray, took the students for relief work during the great Damodar floods. There Meghnad gained firsthand experience of the extent of havoc and misery a flooded river can cause. He had some idea of floods since he came from a land of overflowing rivers, but the Damodar floods proved an eye-opener. Here was untapped energy which, if properly harnessed, could probably be put to great use, he thought. He completed his Bachelor's in mathematics and Master's in mixed mathematics and ranked second, securing first class in both the examinations. At Calcutta (now, Kolkata), he had to eke out a sustenance from a pittance. He was a boarder at the Eden Hindu Hostel, but soon circumstances forced him to quit. He was determined to turn a blind eye to the humiliation inflicted by the 'upper class' boys who went to the extent of not allowing him to eat with them. But, apart from a growing hatred towards Hindu orthodoxy, he never gave vent to his indignation. Over and above the stipend, Meghnad took a few private tuitions which took care of him and his younger brother Kanai.

On the successful completion of his Master of Science, Meghnad joined the University of Calcutta as Lecturer in the

Department of Applied Mathematics under Professor Ganesh Prasad. But soon he was shifted to the physics department. Since Meghnad knew the German language, he along with his friend and colleague Bose, translated Einstein's 'Theory of Relativity' and had it published by the University in 1919. This happened to be the first English translation of the theory of relativity. He then started his research work on the basis of the knowledge acquired from his own private studies. There was no experimental laboratory in the physics department. The only redeeming feature was the rich, well-equipped library of Presidency College. His first research papers were followed by others in quick succession. 'On Maxwell's Stresses'—a study on the electromagnetic theory of radiation—was published in *Philosophical Magazine*, in 1917. On the basis of these papers, he submitted his thesis in 1918 and was awarded Doctor of Science by the University of Calcutta in 1919. He was awarded the Premchand Roychand Studentship in 1919 on the basis of his dissertation, 'On the Harvard Classification of Stellar Spectra'. His thesis 'On the Origin of Lines in Stellar Spectra' was awarded the Griffith Prize of the University of Calcutta in 1920.

On 16 June 1918, Meghnad married Radharani Roy. Though Radharani did not have much formal education, she had a receptive mind and learnt a lot from the varied interests of her husband. The couple had three sons and four daughters.

Meghnad's work on thermal ionisation was not only a major breakthrough in Indian science, but also opened the doors to an almost virgin field of astrophysics, which was hitherto a closed territory. The 'Theory of Ionisation' explained in detail the solar chromosphere, but the problem of corona and coronium remained unsolved. Years later, in 1942, he published a paper titled 'Of a Physical Theory of the Solar Corona'. The money obtained through the Premchand

Roychand Studentship coupled with the patronage given by the Brahmo Education Society enabled him to take a trip to Europe for further research. In England, Meghnad Saha had an opportunity to work in Professor Fowler's laboratory. At the latter's instance, Meghnad Saha went to Germany. He was there for a year conducting experiments on his theory. He met leading physicists like Einstein, Planck and others. He was invited to Munich to deliver a lecture. He spent a month in Switzerland.

In response to an urgent call from Sir Asutosh, Meghnad Saha returned to Calcutta to join as the Khaira Professor of Physics, but, unfortunately, the governor did not approve Sir Asutosh's plans for expansion. However, later Meghnad Saha was appointed Professor and Head of the Department of Physics in Allahabad University. There, he built up a school of gifted students. Very soon, research papers started appearing from Meghnad Saha and his students and the physics department began to throb with new life and enthusiasm. In 1926, he presided over the physics and mathematics sections of the Indian Science Congress. The following year, in 1927, he was elected Fellow of the Royal Society, London. In the same year, the Italian government invited him to the Volta centenary celebrations. On his way to London to attend the Royal Society meeting he went to Lake Como, Italy, to attend the Volta Centenary Conference. It was an exceptional assembly of physicists and electro-technicians of the world for a week-long congress organised in honour of the Italian scientist Volta. On his way back from London, he joined a total solar eclipse expedition to Ringebu in Norway, led by Professor L. Vegard of Oslo University.

At Allahabad, Meghnad Saha continued to work on thermal ionisation and astrophysics. He also initiated and organised research in several other branches of physics, such as statistical mechanics, atomic and molecular spectroscopy, electron affinity of electronegative elements, active modification of nitrogen, high temperature dissociation of molecules, propagation of radio waves in the ionosphere, and physics of the upper atmosphere. At the invitation of Patna University, he delivered a series of lectures on atomic physics. He revised his lecture notes and published them in a monograph, *Six Lectures in Atomic Physics*, from Allahabad University in 1931.

In 1930, Professor Saha was elected the first president of the U.P. Academy of Science. The membership of the Academy soon extended far beyond the geographical limits of the United Provinces of Oudh and Agra. In 1934, the U.P. Academy was renamed the National Academy of Sciences. Around November 1934, Professor Saha delivered special memorial lectures on neutron—the newly discovered elementary nuclear particle. He presented his paper on 'The Origin of Mass in Neutrons and Protons' before the Indian Physical Society on 8 February 1936. He described a method of calculating the pole strength of magnetic monopoles from fundamental principles. This was published in *Indian Journal of Physics* (Vol 10) in 1936. He became the second president of the National Institute of Sciences of India for the term 1937–39. Since its inception, he regularly contributed research papers and took keen interest in the affairs of the Institute till the end. The National Institute of Sciences has now been renamed as the Indian National Science Academy. Gradually, Professor Saha became a powerful force on the scientific scene in India.

Professor Saha's next move was the formation of the Indian Science News Association at Calcutta and the publication of the journal *Science & Culture* on the model of the popular *Nature* of England. In 1936, he undertook an extensive tour of the laboratories in Europe and USA on a fellowship of the Carnegie Trust of the British Empire. There he had an opportunity to acquaint himself with the latest happenings in the West. In Munich, he realised the immense potential of nuclear physics. New and exciting discoveries were being made every day. He spent one month at Oxford and then proceeded to the Harvard College Observatory at Cambridge, Massachusetts. During his stay in Cambridge, he published a paper, 'On a Stratospheric Astrophysical Laboratory'. He predicted that if the solar spectrum could be studied above the ozone layer of the atmosphere, Lyman lines of hydrogen would be found in emission. This was verified eighteen years later by sending V2 rockets in space.

In July 1938, Professor Saha was back in the University of Calcutta as Palit Professor and Head of the Department of Physics. The first thing he did was to remodel the post-graduate syllabus in physics. Just after the discovery of fission in 1939, he introduced a general and a special paper in nuclear physics in 1940. A general paper in quantum mechanics was also added. Now he decided to work in nuclear physics. He visited the Radiation Laboratory of Lawrence at Berkeley, USA, where accelerators were being used to speed up particles. He was able to convince Jawaharlal Nehru, the then Prime Minister of India, of the possibilities of nuclear energy. Nehru shared the same scientific outlook on the future industrialisation of the country. Professor Saha was appointed a member of the Board of Scientific and Industrial Research. Nehru persuaded the Tata Trust to provide the funds needed to set up a cyclotron laboratory. Thus, with the efforts of Professor Saha, the Institute of Nuclear Physics was established on 21 April 1948 and was formally opened on 11 January 1950. Almost simultaneously, the Atomic Energy Commission Act was passed in 1948 and the Atomic Energy

Commission was formed in 1949 with Homi J. Bhabha as Chairman. The Institute along with its post-Master of Science course was a new concept and a new experiment, as Professor Saha wanted it to function as an autonomous body within the framework of the university. The Institute attracted scientists and students from all over India, thus providing a scientific leadership which the Tata Institute of Fundamental Research was to take up later.

In 1952, Professor Saha was appointed a fulltime Director of the re-constituted Indian Association for the Cultivation of Science. He was the Honorary Director of the Institute of Nuclear Physics (renamed as Saha Institute of Nuclear Physics after his death). He held this post till his death in 1956. He was a member of the University Education Commission appointed by the Government of India in 1948 of which Dr Sarvepalli Radhakrishnan was the Chairman. Since the formation of the Board of Scientific Research in 1941, later named the Council of Scientific and Industrial Research (CSIR), he was associated with its activities. He was a member of the governing body and member of other committees formed by it and contributed substantially to its work and growth. He took a leading part in the establishment of the Glass and Ceramic Research Institute at Calcutta. He was also involved in the affairs of the Indian Physical Society and *Indian Journal of Physics*, where some of his significant papers were published. He also took great interest in the functioning of the Asiatic Society. As its president for one term, he tried to revitalise its activities. He was a trustee of the Victoria Memorial of Calcutta, president of the Indo-Soviet Friends Society and vice-president of the Sino-Indian Cultural Association.

When Professor Saha found that the river projects were not being managed properly and it was no longer possible for

him to limit his protests to the fiery editorials of *Science &
Culture*, in 1952 he contested parliamentary election as an
independent candidate from the Calcutta north-west
constituency. He was elected Member of Parliament. From
1952 till his death in 1956 he was an active parliamentarian.
He hit out at the poor performance of the government.
Professor Saha initiated the debate in Parliament on the
peaceful use of nuclear energy on 12 May 1954. This was a
subject very dear to his heart. He presented a strong case for
developing nuclear power in India and provided ample details
of the money other countries were spending for undertaking
this task. He was bitterly critical of the Atomic Energy
Commission and its slow and secretive style of working. He
wanted the Atomic Energy Act to be scrapped altogether and
the Commission to be reorganised in a broad-based manner.
His brief span in Parliament was quite eventful. His criticism
was directed at the government's policies regarding university
education, multipurpose river projects and large-scale
industrialisation. Professor Saha's passion for ancient Indian
history and his love for astronomy found a harmonious fusion
in the reform of the Indian calendar. He critically examined
the method of time reckoning from the ancient times not
only in India but also in other ancient civilisations. His efforts
led to the formation of the Calendar Reform Committee in
1952 by the CSIR, which was headed by Professor Saha. His
prime passion was to see rational thinking operating at every
level of the society.

In spite of his numerous preoccupations, Professor Saha
maintained his links with his village. After Independence,
when East Bengal became another country and streams of
refugees started pouring in, it was like a personal tragedy to
him. As president of the East Bengal Refugee Relief
Committee, he visited the camps of Assam to get firsthand

knowledge of how the government policy of rehabilitation was working. He urged the Prime Minister to integrate the two departments of Planning and Refugee Rehabilitation. As a Member of Parliament, he laid stress on the reorganisation of the States on linguistic basis. On 16 February 1956, he was due to meet Dr J.C. Ghosh at the office of the Planning Commission in Delhi. He paid his taxi-driver and turned to move towards the Rashtrapati Bhavan with some files under his arms. When only a few yards away from the gate he collapsed on the ground. He was rushed to the nearby Willingdon Hospital where doctors declared him dead. It was the day of the Saraswati *puja*. In Calcutta, all festivities came to a halt as thousands thronged the streets to give a befitting farewell to the man who lived and died as a crusader for a valiant cause.

Life for Professor Meghnad Saha had never been a bed of roses. He had struggled hard. The secret of his success as a scientist was his inquisitive mind and clarity of thought. His early training in mathematics may have had a lot to do with this. He never expressed an opinion unless he had studied the pros and cons of the subject. He was a well-read man who had studied the Vedas, the Upanishads, the Puranas and all the Hindu astronomical texts, but was opposed to ritual-based religion of any kind. Though he had a forceful personality, the allegiance he inspired from his students was equally strong. He always believed that they alone are to be regarded as real teachers who can show by experiments what they teach. He himself achieved his highest fulfilment as a teacher because of his sterling qualities of integrity and honesty.

Satyendra Nath Bose

Satyendra Nath Bose, a man of extraordinary intellectual ability, was a distinguished Indian scientist. A versatile genius, in addition to physics and mathematics, his interests embraced such diverse fields as chemistry, mineralogy, social science, philosophy and the languages. He is associated primarily with what came to be known as Bose–Einstein statistics, and Bosons. He blossomed at a time when education in India was not science-oriented, but confined primarily to philosophy, literature, logic and history. It had only just been realised that modern science should be a part of the curriculum, forcing the authorities to introduce the teaching of science. Hence, proper facilities for pursuing science subjects were yet to be developed.

Satyendra Nath Bose was born in Calcutta (now Kolkata) on 1 January 1894 in a high caste Kayastha family with two generations of English education behind them. He was the son of Surendra Nath Bose, an accountant in the executive engineering department of the East India Railway, and Amodini Devi, the daughter of a renowned lawyer. Satyendra Nath possessed in-born talent and had a congenial atmosphere to develop. Whenever his father went out, he gave his son arithmetic sums on the cemented floor of a room which was used as a store. Here, young Satyen would go on writing numbers to his heart's content. It was a kind of game which kept the child out of mischief.

Satyen's schooling began at the age of five. He was admitted in Normal School, and when the family moved to another area, he joined the New Indian School and later Hindu School. A voracious reader, his favourite poets were Alfred Tennyson and Rabindranath Tagore. He was particularly fond of Tennyson's *In Memoriam* and could recite the entire poem from memory. He also knew Kalidasa's *Meghdoot* by heart. He was very good in mathematics. Apart from working out all the sums from the prescribed books, Satyen would solve similar sums from subsidiary textbooks. He was due to sit for his entrance examination in 1908, but unfortunately he came down with an attack of chickenpox just two days prior to the examination. As a result, he lost one year. But he took this opportunity to study advanced mathematics and Sanskrit classics.

Satyen used to do most of his study at night by the light of an earthen lamp. In the entrance examination of 1909, Satyen stood fifth in order of merit. Though he did very well in Sanskrit, history and geography, he opted for the science course. He joined the intermediate science classes at Presidency College, Calcutta. For his Bachelor of Science, he opted for mixed mathematics and scored first class in the university. The same result was repeated in the Master of Science mixed mathematics examination in 1915, while in college he had been devoting a good deal of his time in coaching his classmates and junior friends. He had a natural aptitude for languages. He started taking lessons in French from a French lady as early as 1908. By 1911, he came in contact with the Bhattacharjee brothers, Pashupati and Girija, who were music lovers. Through this association, Satyen received his first training in music and the *esraj* became his first musical instrument. He composed various *ragas* by permutation and combination of notes. While still in his third year, Satyen became the editor of a handwritten journal, *Manisha* (Intellect). One of the stories written by the editor was about his experiences in the jungles of Assam where his father lived, and which he used to visit during the holidays. The treatment showed considerable skill. Later, he was involved in a quarterly called *Parichay*, and a number of cultural groups.

In 1914, at the age of twenty, while still pursuing his Master's, he was married to Ushabati, daughter of a renowned medical practitioner. Their first child, daughter Nilima, was born in 1916. Satyen started giving private tuition to a young prince of the Gauripur estate, Pramathesh Barua, who later became a renowned film director and actor. Satyen was appointed lecturer in the Applied Mathematics Department of Presidency College. Simultaneously, he studied modern physics on his own. He also took German language lessons. He became close to a German Professor, P.J. Bruhl, who did his doctorate in botany but switched over to physics. Bruhl proved an inspiring and sympathetic friend to Bose. Bruhl gave him all his textbooks in physics, which were in German. Satyen was already close to Meghnad Saha who had also learnt the German tongue. Saha and Satyen divided the subjects. Saha was to specialise in thermodynamics and statistical mechanics, and Satyen was to focus on electromagnetism and relativity. Satyen's first research paper on 'The Influence of the Finite Volume of Molecules on the Equation of State' was written jointly with Meghnad Saha. This paper was published in *Philosophical Magazine* (London) in 1918. Satyendra Nath Bose's next two papers 'The Stress Equations of Equilibrium' and 'The Horpol Hode' were published in *Bulletin of the Calcutta Mathematical Society* in 1919 and 1920 respectively.

Both these papers were based purely on mathematical problems. In 1920, Bose's paper on 'The Deduction of Rydberg's Law from the Quantum Theory of Spectral Emission' was published in *Philosophical Magazine*. Bose collaborated with Saha in translating Albert Einstein's papers on the theory of relativity from the original German, which happened to be the first English version of the celebrated German papers.

When Dacca University was founded in 1921, Bose was brought to work in the Physics Department. In Dacca, in spite of the fact that the Dacca University Library was yet to be furnished with the latest journals, Bose continued his research. Within three years, his paper on 'Planck's Law and Light Quantum Hypothesis' was published in *Philosophical Magazine*. Its German translation, by Einstein himself, was published in a scientific journal *Zeitschrift fur Physik*. This won Bose wide acclaim. Within a short time, Bose was ready with another paper, 'Thermal Equilibrium in Radiation Field in Presence of Matter'. He sent its copy to Einstein. Einstein translated it and published it in *Zeitschrift fur Physik* in 1923. Einstein's comments on his paper provided Bose the opportunity to go to Europe for two years.

At the age of twenty-nine, Bose arrived in Paris in October 1924, where he was introduced to the famous French physicist Paul Langevin. Langevin was a student of Pierre Curie, and also the head of the Municipal School where radium was discovered. He also met Madame Curie who asked him to learn French to work in her laboratory. After a few months, Bose worked in the Radium Institute for some time. He was drawn towards X-ray structure analysis. He was also introduced to the famous de Broglie brothers who were doing original researches in X-ray crystallography. This helped Bose establish an X-ray crystallography laboratory at Dacca University on his return. After spending one year in France and working with the luminaries of modern physics, Bose left for Berlin.

In 1926, Satyendra Nath Bose returned to Dacca and was elevated to the post of Professor of Physics. There he organised a modern laboratory, an up-to-date workshop, and a suitable library. He did not confine himself merely to the subject of his specialisation, mathematical physics, but encouraged his colleagues and students to undertake experimental work and helped them with new ideas, both in theory and in experiment. He invited eminent scientists like C.V. Raman and Meghnad Saha. All this helped create an atmosphere of learning and scientific attitude. In 1929, Bose delivered the presidential address of the physics and mathematics sections of the Indian Science Congress and spoke on 'Tendencies in Modern Theoretical Physics'. In 1944, he became the General President of the Indian Science Congress where his presidential address 'The Classical Determinism and the Quantum Theory' was unique and thought-provoking. While in Dacca University, he continued to inspire and foster creativity among his students.

In 1945, Bose was back to his *alma mater*, the University of Calcutta, as a Khaira Professor. In this capacity, he set up a laboratory of organic chemistry in the Department of Pure Physics at the University College of Science. His major contribution was the work on inorganic complex salts and clay minerals. A large number of samples of clay, shale and soil from different parts of India were studied. X-ray diffraction methods and differential thermal analysis were employed in order to understand the atomic structure of common clay minerals. He became President of the Indian Physical Society for the period 1945–48. He also became President of the National Institute of Science for the period 1948–50. Although basically a theoretical physicist, he took keen interest in experiments. In 1954, at the Crystallographic Conference in Paris, he presented a paper describing a new and very significant thermo-luminescence analyser developed by students under his guidance. From 1951, he had been visiting Europe almost every year and the time became ripe for his genius to strike again. His papers on Unified Field Theory, explaining both the Electromagnetic Theory and the General Theory of Relativity were published. They had the unmistakable stamp of his originality and lucidity in the subject.

In 1952, Professor Satyendra Nath Bose was nominated a member of the Rajya Sabha and he continued in this capacity till 1958. In 1954, the Government of India honoured him with the title of Padma Vibhushan. In 1956, at the age of sixty-two, he retired from the post of Khaira Professor, and became Vice-Chancellor of Visva-Bharati University. During his brief stay at Santiniketan, Professor Bose endeared himself to everybody. He drew up a plan for re-organising the existing setup and to introduce a science course. Visva-Bharati then offered a science course only up to the intermediate level. His scheme outlined three stages in the teaching programme. The first stage (age-group 6–11) was earmarked for primary school leaving certificate examination, the second stage (age-group 11–17) for high school leaving certificate examination equivalent to the present intermediate standard, and the third stage (age-group 17–22) was for higher study and research leading to the three-year Bachelor of Arts (Honours) and Master of Arts degrees. It recommended the abolition of the system of matriculation and Bachelor of Arts (Pass) examination. It also provided for training in almost all the important Indian, Asian and European languages, both modern and classical. A science institute was proposed to be set up for teaching and research in some of the important branches of physics and biology. He shared with Rabindranath Tagore the theory that basic education should be imparted through the mother tongue. In 1959, he left Visva-Bharati and returned to Calcutta and the scientific world.

A number of honours and academic distinctions came his way. In 1957, three universities—Calcutta, Jadavpur and Allahabad—conferred on him honorary doctorate degrees. The University of Calcutta appointed him Emeritus Professor in 1957 and allowed him to retain his office for holding seminars and discussions at the main building of the University College of Science and Technology, the office he was occupying as Khaira Professor of Physics. His purpose was to make an intensive study of theoretical developments in nuclear physics in order to obtain greater insight into the nature of the fundamental particles and the laws of interaction. He sponsored the scheme for making a systematic analysis of spring water and supervised the construction of a field laboratory at Bakreswar. In 1958 he was elected a Fellow of the Royal Society of London, and in 1959 he was appointed National Professor, the highest honour conferred by the nation upon a scholar. In 1961, after he had left the place, Visva-Bharati conferred upon him the title of 'Desikottama'. His seventieth birthday was celebrated by his students and admirers. The Science Congress, held that year, had a seminar on Bose Statistics and Unified Field Theory in his honour. The Delhi University observed his seventieth birthday with a seminar on 'Forty Years of Bose Statistics' and presented him a collection of articles on Bosons, edited by R.C. Mazumdar. This volume contained a number of papers illustrating the great impact which Bose's work made on contemporary physics. In 1974, when he became an octogenarian, celebrations were organised nationwide. The year coincided with the golden jubilee of Bose Statistics. An international seminar was held at Calcutta and was attended by scientific celebrities from all over the world.

Professor Bose visited Europe again. In 1953, he was asked to attend the World Congress for General Disarmament and Peace at Budapest. Invitations came from Soviet Russia,

Denmark and Czechoslovakia. He visited Geneva, Paris, Copenhagen, Zurich and Prague. The following year, he attended the International Crystallography Conference in Paris as a representative from India. Apart from scientific interests, he had a special liking for France and the French way of life. The year 1955 saw him in Paris again, this time on an invitation from the Council of National Scientific Research of France. He went to England in 1956 to attend the Annual Meeting of the British Association for the Cultivation of Science.

Two years later, Professor Bose was back in London to attend the Royal Society meeting where he was nominated a Fellow. In 1962, he went to Sweden and from there to Moscow to attend the Peace Conference. In August 1962, he was invited to Japan to attend a seminar on 'The Role of Science in Modern Life'. It was an international seminar and Bose had naturally expected that the deliberations would be carried out in English. But he was told that in spite of the fact that most Japanese scientists understood English and a few other languages, the entire education in the country was conducted in Japanese. Bose was greatly impressed by the effectiveness of this method. A most technical, abstract and complicated exchange was carried on in Japanese and the audience had no difficulty in catching the gist of what was said, which was evident from the sharp criticisms that followed. Bose went to Japanese universities to enquire about the details. He saw that the Japanese always discussed the latest scientific ideas in their mother tongue. After his return to Calcutta, this idea of a vernacular-based science education became his mission. He spoke endlessly on the subject to students, teachers and the general public. It was the theme of his convocation address in 1962. His passion for developing science and scientific writing in Bengali extended even to abstruse subjects like hydrodynamics and physics.

January 1974 was a hectic one for Professor Bose. He had to attend a number of receptions, seminars and exhibitions and felt tired. Speaking at a seminar, he spoke of his long years of struggle and the satisfaction at having seen his life's work appreciated at long last. 'Now I feel I do not need to live any longer,' his words ended with a ring of prophecy. On 4 February 1974, after an attack of bronchial pneumonia, this creative life came to an end in the early hours. By afternoon, the Goabagan boys' library had badges printed and pinned on the shirts of all the members with these words in Bengali: 'Our homage to the undying lamp'. Children and adults poured in to have a last glimpse of the body kept in the portico of the Science College. Though Professor Bose was well advanced in years, and his death was, by no means, unexpected, the public expression of sorrow was spontaneous and overwhelming. They were all proud of the legend that was Satyen Bose.

Satyendra Nath Bose endeared himself to people—even to the man on the street not concerned with physics. Mathematics and physics were not his only concerns. He was loving and sociable. He was loyal and devoted to friends to such an extent that these relationships provided him the greatest emotional sustenance through difficult times. His quality to interact and mix with people endeared him to everybody with whom he came in contact. Vanity and pride had absolutely no place in his temperament despite his great achievements. Apart from mathematics and physics, Bose also found time to indulge in literary activities. He went to the literary meetings known as 'Bichitra', conducted by Tagore. In his later years, when Professor Bose could not walk out of the house, his home became a meeting place of his friends—literary get-togethers—where the topics discussed ranged across science, history and philosophy. From the way Professor Bose talked, it seemed that he was an expert on every subject, and not just his own.

Homi Jehangir Bhabha

'For the full industrialisation of the underdeveloped areas and for the continuation of our civilisation and its further development, atomic energy is not merely an aid, it is an absolute necessity. . . . The immediate nuclear power programme is the seed from which can grow the tree of a large and increasing power programme based on plutonium and ultimately thorium,' observed Dr Homi J. Bhabha just after India's Independence in 1947. His observation was based on a complete survey of the resources of power production in India and he proved that the established reserves of oil and coal in India were insufficient to meet our requirements. He maintained that the large-scale industrialisation of the country and the raising of the standard of living of our people to a level comparable to that of the industrially advanced countries could be achieved only through an extensive utilisation of nuclear energy. Though Western in his upbringing—he was fed on a diet of Beethoven, Chopin, Shakespeare, a culture entailing the use of knives and forks—he was a man of the renaissance that ushered in Independence in India.

Bhabha found that India has the largest reserves of thorium in the world, of the order of 500,000 tons of ore containing 9 per cent thorium. Thorium, he found, is easily extracted from the ore and so the refined material would be available at a much lower price than that of uranium elsewhere in the world. Since the thorium by itself cannot be used to start a power programme, natural uranium must also be used, and we have to find ways of utilising thorium subsequently for increasing nuclear power capacity. Thorium itself cannot be fissioned to give useful energy. This can be converted, when placed in reactors, into another form of uranium, U-233, which is a concentrated nuclear fuel, like plutonium or U-235. He proposed a solution to this problem. Plutonium, which is a fissile material, is generated in natural uranium, which can be used for fuelling stations of the appropriate type. Such power stations must be regarded as dual purpose power stations, which will not only produce electricity at an economic or near economic rate, but will also produce this most valuable fuel, plutonium. The plutonium can then be used in plutonium–thorium reactors, which produce energy as well as U-233. Finally, the U-233 can be used in U-233 thorium reactors. These reactors would produce more U-233 than they consume. Then they would need a continuous feed of thorium alone. This way, he felt, we, in India, can achieve self-sufficiency in atomic fuels.

Dr Bhabha calculated that for a power station of 380-megawatt capacity, 10,00,000 tons of coal would be required every year, whereas the same amount of power can be achieved with only 25 tons of uranium. Thus, it was through Dr Bhabha's efforts that India started building the first atomic power station at Tarapur on the Maharashtra–Gujarat border with the help of an American firm. Another one at Rana Pratap Sagar in Rajasthan with Canadian aid followed. The third atomic power station was built at Kalpakkam near Madras (now Chennai), entirely by Indian scientists and engineers. Thus, Dr Homi Jehangir Bhabha became the 'Father of Nuclear Energy' in India.

Born in a Parsi family on 30 October 1909, Homi Jehangir Bhabha was the son of J.H. Bhabha, the famous lawyer and consultant to the Tata Company in Bombay (now, Mumbai) and his wife Meherbai. J.H. Bhabha was a man of culture who had studied in England. The Bhabhas were thrilled when their first-born was a son. The boy was brought up with great care and love. Homi loved music since his early childhood. It so happened that one day, when he was crying, the music playing from the adjoining room was only able to control him. He loved listening to records of great musicians from all over the world. The great European composer, Beethoven, was his favourite. Homi could remember every note and rhythm of the music. He could repeat the tunes without any effort.

Homi was gifted with a keen mind. In his childhood he used to sleep very little, causing great worry to his parents who consulted experienced and qualified doctors. But the doctors were unable to diagnose the reason. This upset the parents greatly. Ultimately, they took the child to a European doctor who thoroughly examined the child and reported that there was no need to worry about his health. The cause of his sleeping much less, the doctor reported, was only his super-active brain through which thoughts ran endlessly. In his childhood, Homi gained proficiency in painting and drawing. He was very fond of nature. Homi's parents were keen to give him the best possible education. He was sent to Cathedral and John Canon High School at Bombay where he proved to be a bright student. He was not interested in games, but developed his interest in 'Meccano' which required him to join blocks. This helped him build up his concentration powers. He loved books and spent hours at a stretch in his school and home libraries. He also set up a small laboratory in his home library and tried out experiments after reading books. At fifteen, he could understand Einstein's Theory of Relativity.

Homi's parents decorated their home library with a number of paintings of great artists. Homi often gazed at them for hours. This inspired him to start painting on his own. He bought colours, paint brush and canvas and started his first painting without telling anybody at home. This he gave to his mother on her birthday as a surprise gift. As Homi grew older, his tender feelings turned to nature. The plants and flowers excited him and he painted scenes of nature. He also took painting lessons from a renowned artist in Bombay. At fifteen, he passed the Senior Cambridge examination and joined Elephinston College. Music and painting continued as his hobbies.

Homi was interested in physics and mathematics. But his father wanted him to become an engineer. He was sent to Cambridge University for an engineering course. In England, in addition to his regular study in mechanical engineering, he found time to attend musical programmes and continued painting. He visited famous art galleries. One can still find his paintings in some art galleries of London. After passing the Mechanical Science Tripos in 1930, he was awarded the Rounce Ball travelling studentship in mathematics for two years. He worked with Wolfgang Pauli in Zurich and with Enrico Fermi in Rome during this period. On the expiry of the studentship, he was given the Isaac Newton studentship in 1933 and the 1851 Exhibition studentship in 1936. He was awarded doctorate in science and was appointed professor of physics in the University of Cambridge.

Dr Homi J. Bhabha's first major achievement in physics was the elegant foundation of the theory of production of electron–positron pairs. His theory was based on the observation that when high energy photons interact with any force, they lose energy which is converted into electron–positron pairs. When an electron or positron experiences nuclear forces, it emits electromagnetic radiation or, in other words, high energy photons. This naturally leads to a shower of electrons and positrons from the initial photon. Further work in this theory was done by Dr Bhabha in 1943 while in Bangalore.

As a teacher, Dr Homi J. Bhabha endeared himself to the students by presenting even the most difficult problem in an interesting, systematic and simple manner. He also did some research in 'cosmic rays'. In 1937, he and a German physicist solved the mystery surrounding these rays. He was guided by Nobel laureates like Rutherford and Niels Bohr. He found that 'cosmic rays' had a new particle unknown to scientists. He named these new particles 'mesons'. He used Einstein's Theory of Relativity to prove that as the speed of 'mesons' increases, they live longer. Dr Bhabha was widely acclaimed for his brilliant calculations.

Dr Bhabha had visualised that nuclear energy could be successfully applied for power production well before the first atom bomb wrecked Hiroshima and before nuclear energy became the bandwagon of science. In 1940, when the Second World War started, a number of countries wanted to use Dr Bhabha's knowledge and experience. Germany, at that time, had already produced many weapons of destruction. The major concern of scientists the world over was the study of atoms as sources of enormous destructive power. England and USA decided to utilise Dr Bhabha's knowledge and experience in the field. He was given an American aircraft and full facilities were provided to him for his defence research. Oxford University invited him to join as a Theoretical

Physicist. But he was more concerned with the use of the atom for constructive purposes. At that time, India was under colonial rule and there was not much development in science. The patriotic feelings in Dr Bhabha compelled him to return to India leaving behind the most lucrative job in Cambridge. With a view to attain his objective he joined the Indian Institute of Science at Bangalore. The Nobel laureate Dr C.V. Raman was then its Director. Dr Bhabha continued further research in 'cosmic rays' under Dr Raman's guidance.

In 1941, Dr Bhabha was elected Fellow of the Royal Society of London. The Royal Society provided him financial assistance to undertake experiments and research in new areas of physics. He found that research facilities at that time in India were lacking. In March 1944, Dr Bhabha suggested to the Tata Trustees to set up a research institute to help scientists in India. Scientists all over the world at that time were busy in experimenting with the atom to make bombs. But Dr Bhabha was keen to use the atom for the welfare of mankind. He proposed to the Tatas that the country should have indigenous facilities to train scientists instead of depending on foreign help, and that India should be able to build nuclear plants for power production. The Tata Institute of Fundamental Research (TIFR) was set up in 1945 with this aim in view and Dr Bhabha became its first Director. The Institute became an important milestone in India's progress in the sophisticated field of nuclear science.

Dr Bhabha found that India did not have enough coal and oil to produce energy for a long time. He studied the situation in detail and came to the conclusion that atomic power stations had to be built to generate power. He was able to convince Prime Minister Jawaharlal Nehru in this regard. Traditional power generation centres use coal and oil and are known as thermal power stations. Some, which use water, are called hydro-electric power stations. But in atomic power stations, certain materials like uranium and plutonium are mixed with other substances. The energy thus produced is a million times greater than that obtained from burning coal. Dr Bhabha's suggestion was accepted and the Atomic Energy Commission was set up in 1948 with Dr Bhabha as its Chairman.

Dr Bhabha's continued efforts culminated in the setting up of Asia's first atomic research reactor in 1955, where 200 scientists worked on the project. Under his expert guidance, three reactors were built and were named as Apsara, Circus and Zerlina. The scientists of Trombay set up many high-technology plants. Among them were the thorium and plutonium plants. India became the fifth country to have a plutonium plant. In 1963, work started on the first atomic power station at Tarapore, near Bombay.

In 1962, Dr Bhabha was appointed Chairman of Electronics Committee of the Government of India to suggest ways and means for the advancement of electronics. His report helped the government to set up the Electronics Production Centre. He encouraged the Indian scientists to work hard to match with the best in the world. He also encouraged research in space science, radio, astronomy and microbiology. The radio telescope at Ooty is one of his creations.

Dr Bhabha received invitations to lecture at different universities like Columbia, Edinburgh, Cambridge and Vancouver. At these places, he explained to scientists the progress made by their Indian counterparts. He always maintained that a scientist does not belong to a particular nation but to the whole world, and that the doors of science should be kept open to all those who work for the welfare of humanity. He was for an exchange of information, and brought together many renowned scientists on one platform. This gave the Indian scientists a better chance than before to know the scientific world outside and created self-confidence in them. Once, when a press reporter asked Dr Bhabha about his marriage, he had replied: 'I am married to creativity.' He lived up to that statement. He was not only creative throughout his life, but opened new vistas to young and budding scientists to contribute towards the progress and prosperity of humanity. Originality and inventiveness were the two greatest virtues of Dr Bhabha and he pursued them with ruthless energy and devotion, possessed with an enormous vitality and sense of purpose.

Dr Bhabha derived energy and inspiration from the arts, music, paintings, trees and his beloved roses. To him the arts were what made life worth living. This perhaps was the secret behind his creativity. He wrote and submitted 81 research papers and was appropriately recognised at various forums. In 1944, he was awarded the degree of Doctor of Science by Patna University. In 1948, he received the Hopkin's prize. In 1954, Padma Bhushan was conferred on him by the President of India and in 1961 he was awarded the Meghnad Saha Gold Medal. Universities in Lucknow, Allahabad, Cambridge, London and other places conferred on him the degree of Doctor of Science. In 1964, he was given the Melchett award. But he could not go to England to receive it. It was presented to his mother at her residence after his death.

Dr Homi Jehangir Bhabha dreamed of an India which would be at par with any other country in the world. His keen sense of aesthetics was evident in any task he undertook. When the Tata Institute of Fundamental Research was set up, Dr Bhabha having recognised the potential of M.F. Husain, then relatively unknown, asked him to adorn the building with his works. He wanted to bring the Palace of Versailles to India by creating the Atomic Energy Research Establishment, now known as Bhabha Atomic Research Centre. He believed that ambience played an important role in the workplace. Anything that was haphazard, casual or shoddy would make him passionately angry. While building Apsara, for instance, he ensured that men who worked round the clock had a constant supply of food.

On 24 January 1966, while flying to Geneva to attend an international conference, the aircraft he was travelling in crashed on the Alps. Indian scientists lost their leader, and the country a great patriot and visionary. As a tribute to his legacy, the Atomic Energy Establishment at Trombay was named Bhabha Atomic Research Centre and it observed the day as a working day instead of a holiday in memory of the departed leader. J.R.D. Tata presented a statue of Dr Bhabha to the Tata Institute of Fundamental Research and renamed the road leading to the Institute as Homi Bhabha Marg. The high school where he had his education started a studentship in his memory. Above all, Dr Homi Jehangir Bhabha will be remembered as a great lover of music, a gifted artist, a brilliant engineer and an outstanding scientist.

Subrahmanyan Chandrasekhar

'The simple is the seal of the true, and beauty is the splendour of truth.' These were the concluding words of the Nobel lecture delivered on 8 December 1983 in the Royal Swedish Academy Hall in Stockholm by Subrahmanyan Chandrasekhar, who became a legendary figure for his prolific contributions to astrophysics, physics and applied mathematics. His legend began at the age of nineteen, when he formulated the epochal 'Chandrasekhar Limit' that led to the discovery of neutron stars and black holes. Chandra, as his biographer Kameshwar C. Wali referred to him, pursued research in physics, astrophysics and mathematics, adding to our understanding of the constitution and evolution of stars as well as numerous other aspects of the physical universe.

Born on 19 October 1910, Chandra was the first son of C.S. Ayyar and Sitalakshmi. He had two older sisters, Rajalakshmi (Rajam) and Balaparvathi (Bala). Later, the Ayyars had three more sons. Chandra, as the firstborn son, inherited his paternal grandfather's name: Chandrasekhar. But soon his elders called him 'Ayya', and his younger brothers and sisters, 'Anna'.

Chandra had his primary education in Lahore. He learned Tamil from his mother, and English and arithmetic from his father. As was the practice in middle-class families, Chandra's parents gave initial education to their children at home. At that time, there were few private schools and those were reserved for the children of the ruling British or well-to-do princes, *maharajas*, or their surrogates. Schools run by Christian missions concentrated their efforts on the poor and the lower castes, easier targets for conversion to Christianity. However, Chandra's home education was disciplined. He enjoyed learning English, and arithmetic caught his fancy very early. Chandra's father was amazed at the abilities of his child. Chandra followed the footsteps of his uncle, C.V. Raman, who exhibited precocious brilliance in school and college.

In 1918, the family moved to Madras (now, Chennai). At the age of eleven, Chandra was admitted to Hindu High School in Triplicane where his performance was so brilliant that others, who did not compete, became envious or had grudges. All the people considered him a genius. His interest in mathematics was evident from the beginning as he used to do an incredibly large number of mathematical problems every day. In 1924, the family moved to their newly constructed house, known as Chandra Vilas, near Dr Sarvepalli Radhakrishnan's house. His private studies in mathematics put him far ahead of his classmates and he invariably received the highest grades in his class. After completing his intermediate at Presidency College with distinction in physics, chemistry and mathematics, he came under the spell of the legendary mathematician, Srinivasa Ramanujan. He was ten years old when Ramanujan expired. After hearing and reading about Ramanujan, he was determined to pursue mathematics for his Bachelor's degree, but to please his father he officially registered himself as a student of physics. In the summer of

1927, he read Arnold Sommerfield's *Atomic Structure and Spectral Lines*, a classic treatise on the quantum theory of the atom. Though officially a student of physics honours, Chandra also attended lectures in the mathematics department.

In 1928, when C.V. Raman along with K.S. Krishnan made a fundamental discovery in the molecular scattering of light, Chandra heard him explain the effect and heard others rank it with the Compton Effect, for which Arthur Holly Compton had received the Nobel Prize in 1927. Soon afterwards, Chandra went to Calcutta (now, Kolkata) to spend the summer months working in the very laboratory where the discovery was made. Raman wanted to give his young nephew a start in experimental work and asked him to assist one of his senior research scientists working on X-ray diffraction by liquids. Raman took him for occasional ferry rides down the river Hooghly and talked to him about his discovery. Thus inspired, Chandra returned to Madras to begin his second year of undergraduate studies. In 1928, when Sommerfield visited Madras Chandra met him. Sommerfield had studied the behaviour of electrons inside a metal, applying the newly discovered quantum statistics of Fermi and Dirac. Chandra wrote a paper within a few months entitled, 'The Compton Scattering and the New Statistics' and had it published in *Proceedings of the Royal Society* with the help of Ralph Howard Fowler.

In 1929, Chandra studied the effect of magnetic field on Compton Scattering and prepared a short paper for publication in *Indian Journal of Physics* while he was still an eighteen-year-old undergraduate student. While he was in the final year, Chandra had an opportunity to receive Werner Heisenberg of Germany, a pioneer in quantum mechanics, and take him to Kanchipuram and Mahabalipuram temples around Madras. Chandra then utilised this opportunity to discuss his papers with Heisenberg. A few months later, in January 1930, he attended the Indian Science Congress Association in Allahabad and met Meghnad Saha, the eminent Indian astrophysicist known for his theory of ionisation. Saha had unlocked the door to the interpretation of stellar spectra in terms of laboratory spectra of atoms of terrestrial elements, providing information about the state of stellar atmospheres, their chemical composition, the density distribution of various elements, and then about that most important physical parameter—the temperature. Saha complemented Chandra for his paper in *Proceedings of the Royal Society*.

Within days of his return from attending the Science Congress in Allahabad, Chandra was offered a Government of India scholarship to pursue his research in England. Before this, his two papers were also published in *Philosophical Magazine*. Suddenly his mother fell ill and he was reluctant to leave her in such a condition. But he was encouraged by her to stick to his schedule. Chandra wanted admission in Trinity College, Cambridge, to work under Fowler for doctoral research, but a week before his planned departure he received a cable informing him that it was not possible to get admission to Cambridge and that he should think of joining University College, London. He wrote to the concerned authorities and requested them to look into the matter again. Hoping for the best, he proceeded as planned and left Madras for Bombay on 22 July 1930 arriving in London on 19 August 1930.

In England, on the strength of a personal letter from Fowler, Chandra was admitted to Trinity. There he worked hard and continued to do research on his own, submitted papers for publication, and attended lectures. His research efforts won him election to the 'Sheep Shanks Exhibition' and an associated award of forty pounds. It was a special honour bestowed every year to a candidate for proficiency in astrophysics. He was introduced to the Royal Astronomical Society, London, where he regularly contributed papers and, at times, presented his work. He made stellar models which required every star to have a degenerate core obeying one equation of state surrounded by outer layers of stellar material obeying the perfect gas equation of state. He had taken the idea of a degenerate core from Fowler's work on white dwarfs. The results were published in *Astrophysical Journal in America*. He went to Copenhagen in 1932 and discussed his work with Leon Rosenfeld.

At the International Astronomical Union meeting of 1935 held in Paris, Eddington proclaimed that Chandrasekhar's work was heresy; there was no such thing as relativistic degeneracy. Every star, no matter what it was, had a finite state, and the idea of a limiting mass was an absurdity. Chandra had no resources to counter Eddington's influence. The theoretical reasoning of Eddington was too complicated for most astronomers to follow, but his style and prestige were sufficient to convince most of them that he might be right. Chandra felt a psychological impediment to go on working and publishing things which, he knew, people were going to ignore or consider erroneous. Still he worked out a number of things, for example, the theory of rotating white dwarfs. In 1939, he was invited to an international meeting in Paris where Eddington was also invited. There he gave a complete account of his theory with full numerical details. He again enunciated the significance of his results on the prevailing notions of stellar evolution. There was some discussion. This was the last meeting when Chandra and Eddington met face to face. Soon thereafter, the Second World War broke out and Eddington died in 1944. But Chandra still retained the highest admiration for Eddington. In his obituary speech at the University of Chicago, Chandra described Eddington next to Karl Schwarzschild as the greatest astronomer of his time.

It took nearly three decades before the full significance of his discovery was recognised and the 'Chandrasekhar Limit' entered the standard lexicon of physics and astrophysics. Before this, Chandra had a discouraging experience and astronomers took him as Don Quixote trying to kill Eddington. Sometime he thought that it is better to change the topic. But this traumatic event became a turning point in Chandra's life. It had a 'sobering effect'; he became inward bound. The relentless mastery of a certain area and, once mastered, the ability to leave it entirely for another, became Chandra's hallmark in his scientific pursuits.

At the instance of Cambridge University Press, Chandra wrote a small book on stellar atmospheres in the *Cambridge Mathematical Tracts* series. This brought him an opportunity to spend a year in USA at Yale and Harvard. There, his successful lectures prompted Shapley to nominate Chandra as a candidate for election to the 'Society of Fellows'. If elected by the Harvard faculty, he would be a Fellow for three years and the fellowship was worth $2,700 per year, inclusive of rooms in the college and dinner. It would also allow him to pursue his research in complete freedom. Concurrently, he received an invitation from Otto Struve of the Yerkes Observatory to visit Yerkes and 'give some lectures under the auspices of the University of Chicago'. He also received from Struve an offer of a research associateship at Yerkes with a starting salary of $3,000 per year. This sudden interest in him and his work among American astronomers was surprising. In fact, Struve was doing something new in USA. He was bringing young theorists and astronomers together in a place given predominantly to observational work. Therefore, Chandra decided that he would work in USA for at least three years, but in view of the exigencies of some circumstances at home he left for India and was back home in October 1936.

In Madras, Chandra was married to Lalitha on 11 September 1936. She had been working as a scientist in Karaikkudi and shared Chandra's dedication to science. They got to know each other before Chandra left for England and met when they were students in the physics honours course. It was a simple marriage as Chandra's father was averse to the dowry system and the expenses of his daughters' marriages had turned him against such conventional extravaganzas. A one-day ceremony fulfilling all the essential precepts of Hindu rites was performed at the Tirupathi Temple at Tiruchanur near Madras. After spending some time in India the couple left for Cambridge, from where they went to Boston and then Chicago.

In Chicago, Lalitha attended astronomy and astrophysics lectures at the observatory and joined local women's groups. But the responsibilities of taking care of the family were uppermost in her mind and she gave up the idea of further studies. Chandra was elevated to the post of Assistant Professor. Hence, Chandra decided to launch his scientific career at the Yerkes Observatory of the University of Chicago, equipped with the world's largest refracting telescope. His principal assignment was to develop a graduate programme in astronomy and astrophysics. He was put in charge of the library (ordering books and journals), advising students, and arranging the weekly colloquia. His reputation as a teacher and his enthusiasm for research soon attracted students from all parts of the world. His own research and writing continued unabated. In his first year at Yerkes, in addition to writing half a dozen research papers, he completed the manuscript of his first monograph, *An Introduction to the Study of Stellar*

Structure. From 1938 to 1944 his research encompassed work on stellar dynamics, dynamical friction, stochastic problems in physics and astronomy, and the negative hydrogen ion. From 1944 to 1949, his preoccupation was with radiative transfer, culminating in his book, *Radiative Transfer*.

With the onset of the Second World War, Chandra felt anguished and it dampened his exuberance for science. Political upheaval in India, the detention of leaders, and other disturbances perturbed him. Lalitha and Chandra participated in the civilian effort to help the British. On 7 December 1941, while Chandra and Lalitha were still at Princeton, the Japanese struck at Pearl Harbour and USA entered the war. Chandra decided to take the initiative and join the rest of the scientific community, which was unanimously behind the war effort. Von Neumann was engaged in war-related work in the Ballistic Research Laboratory at the Aberdeen Proving Grounds (APG) in Maryland. This laboratory was established during the First World War with a small group of scientists whose task was to study the ballistics of artillery missiles, prepare firing tables for use on the battlefields, and set the elevation of the artillery piece so that the missile could be fired at a certain predetermined range to hit the target. Chandra started working at the APG in February 1943 at a remuneration of thirty dollars per day with travel allowance, and soon became a part of an outstanding group of scientists which included John von Neumann, Ronald Gurney, Joseph Myer, L.H. Thomas, Martin Schwarzschild, Edwin Hubble, Robert Sachs, and many others. He felt stimulated by the novelty of the applied, war-related work, the companionship of scientists from diverse fields, and the feeling of service and sacrifice in the cause of humanity.

Von Neumann attempted to enlist Chandra for the Manhattan project in 1944. Chandra knew about the A-bomb project vaguely. He agreed to the proposal. It seemed that the war would end soon. But somehow the idea was dropped and Chandra did not go to Los Alamos. His own research continued and he produced a steady stream of papers and books. He was promoted to an associate professorship in 1942, followed by a promotion to full professorship in 1943. He was also nominated as a Fellow of the Royal Society of England. The controversy between Chandra and Eddington was a thing of the past now. Warm friendship between the two had prevailed through the war years, and the news of Eddington's death in 1944 distressed Chandra deeply. When the war ended, the process of rebuilding the universities began everywhere. Chandra received an offer of a research professorship from Princeton but declined it. He continued working in the University of Chicago. In 1952, he became the managing editor of *Astrophysical Journal* and continued this work till 1971.

In 1952, Chandra was awarded the Bruce Medal, and he received the Gold Medal of the Royal Astronomical Society in 1953. With the exception of Eddington, no other astronomer had received both these medals by the age of forty-two. Physics began to dominate Chandra's research from 1950 onwards with his work in magneto-hydrodynamics, stability of rotating fluids, plasma physics, and ellipsoidal figures of equilibrium. By 1960, Chandra became more interested in Einstein's General Theory of Relativity and the mathematical study of black holes and colliding waves. Lalitha and Chandra now decided to become naturalised citizens of USA. As a non-citizen, he had often faced difficulties of a bureaucratic nature in fulfilling his scientific obligations. He could not formally invite foreign scientists as visiting lecturers and take care of the necessary procedures on his own. Papers had to be signed by someone else. Every time he left the country, he had to secure an income tax clearance certificate and a re-entry permit. Their trip to India in 1951 had been a moving experience for both of them. On 13 October 1953, Chandra and Lalitha became American citizens.

In 1961, Chandra visited India again. He went around the country giving lectures and spent nearly six months. He met Jawaharlal Nehru at the latter's residence and had dinner with him. In India, National Professorship was offered to him for five years, which could be renewed, but Chandra had other plans. The Padma Vibhushan was conferred on him in 1968. In November 1968, Chandra delivered the Nehru Memorial Lecture, presided over by Prime Minister Indira Gandhi. He talked about the role of astronomy in human culture with particular reference to Hindu culture, and the problems of astronomy and how they reflect on the larger aspects of life.

The announcement of the 1983 Nobel Prize for physics, which Chandra shared with William A. Fowler, was greeted with great joy and appreciation throughout the scientific world. Soon, Chandra was inundated with telephone calls, telegrams, and letters of congratulations and good wishes from his former students, associates, scientists, heads of scientific institutions, and governments. They came from many parts of the world, reflecting his multi-faceted associations. But one could see Chandra going through the Stockholm ceremonies in December 1983 in a rather sombre mood. He appeared to be overwhelmed by it, but not overjoyed. He was proper and dignified, but not relaxed as he received the prize from His Majesty, the King of Sweden. Perhaps, the recognition came to him too late. It was nearly after forty years of the discovery of black holes in the astronomical universe that the Nobel award brought an extremely private and somewhat shy individual into limelight and public attention. On the occasion of a consulate dinner honouring Chandra, a lady asked him, 'The work you are recognised for was apparently done fifty years ago. What have you been doing since?' Chandra responded, 'They also serve who only stand and wait.'

Chandra and Lalitha's life in USA was not without unpleasant incidents. Segregation and colour discrimination brought bitter experiences. But Chandra was already familiar with the racial discrimination in the American society before he had accepted the appointment at Yerkes against the advice of his father and friends in India. His uncle, C.V. Raman, had faced humiliating experiences during his visit to USA in the late 1920s. Chandra was, therefore, prepared for such confrontations. Once, they made reservations in Barbizon Plaza, but when they reached the place they were informed that there was no record of reservation. There was no place for them in the nearby hotel, and then Chandra remembered his uncle, C.V. Raman's experience. When they were about to turn back, his friend helped him get accommodation in another hotel.

Chandra took voluntary retirement in 1980 and ceased to have any teaching or other obligations at the University of Chicago. He was offered post-retirement with essentially no obligation on his part, but he acquitted himself of that privilege as well in 1985. The university converted the post-retirement compensation into a research grant and conferred upon him the emeritus status. Age seemed to have little or no impact on Chandra's fervour for science and the pursuit of the life of the mind. Since his classic work on the mathematical theory of black holes, published in 1983, he pursued the study of colliding waves and the Newtonian two-centre problem in the framework of the general theory of relativity. Apart from science, Chandra had a deep and abiding interest in literature and classical music. He cultivated them with almost the same degree of thoroughness and intensity as his research interests. He systematically read the works of Turgenev, Dostoevsky, Tolstoy, Virginia Woolf, T.S. Eliot, Thomas Hardy, John Galsworthy, Bernard Shaw, Henrik Ibsen and Shakespeare.

Chandra and Lalitha lived near the University of Chicago till Chandra breathed his last on 2 August 1995. They had a comfortable but simple life. Meticulousness dominated Chandra's life and work. Even his rough calculations and draft manuscripts were organised and written so neatly and painstakingly that they appeared to be printed. He is said to be the only scientist in the world who used Gothic symbols in his equations as well as rough calculations. His contribution and dedication to science is an inspiration to the younger as well as ageing scientists.

Bibliography

Basu, S.N., *Jagadish Chandra Bose*, National Book Trust, New Delhi.

Chatterjee, Santimay, *Meghnad Saha*, National Book Trust, New Delhi.

Chatterjee, Santimay, *Satyendra Nath Bose*, National Book Trust, New Delhi.

Deshmukh, Chintamani, *Homi Jehangir Bhabha*, National Book Trust, New Delhi.

Dey, Bishnu, *Satyendra Nath Bose*, Indian Oxygen, Kolkata.

Geddes, Patrick, *Life and Work of Sir Jagadish Chandra Bose*, Asian Education Services, New Delhi.

Gupta, M., *Jagadish Chandra Bose: A Biography*, Bharatiya, Mumbai.

Home, Amal (Ed), *Acharya Jagadish Chandra Bose Birth Centenary 1858-1958*, Acharya Jagadish Chandra Birth Centenary Committee, Kolkata.

Hooda, D.S. & J.N. Kapur, *Aryabhata: Life and Contributions*, 2nd Edition, New Age International, New Delhi.

Jaggi, O.P., *Scientists of Ancient India and Their Achievements*, Atma Ram, Delhi.

Karmohapatro, S.B., *Meghnad Saha*, Publications Div, New Delhi.

Kulkarni, R.P. & V. Sarma, *Homi Bhabha: Father of Nuclear Science in India*, Popular Prakn, Mumbai.

Levy, H., *The Universe of Science*, Rupa & Co, New Delhi.

Murthi, K.R. Srikantha, *Illustrated Susruta Samhita*, Chaukhamba Orientalia, Varanasi.

Murthi, R.K., *Science: Nature's Copycat*, Publications Div, New Delhi.

Naikar, Chandramouli S., *Patanjali of Yogasutras*, Sahitya Akademi, New Delhi.

Narayana Rao, V.S., *Mokshagundam Visvesvaraya*, National Book Trust, New Delhi.

Negular, H.S, *Bharatratan Sir Dr. M. Vishvesvaraya*, Dharwar, Bharat Book Depot.

Prakash, Satya, *Founders of Sciences in Ancient India*, Research Institute of Scientific Studies, Delhi.

Ray, Kamalesh, *Life Work of Meghnad Saha*, NCERT, New Delhi.

Salwi, Dillip M., *C.V. Raman:The Scientist Extraordinary*, Rupa & Co, New Delhi.

Salwi, Dilip M., *Homi J. Bhabha: Architect of Nuclear India*, Rupa & Co, New Delhi.

Salwi, Dilip M., *Jagadish Chandra Bose: The First Modern Scientist*, Rupa & Co, New Delhi.

Salwi, Dilip M., *M.N. Saha: Scientist with a Social Mission*, Rupa & Co, New Delhi.

Salwi, Dilip M., *M. Visvesvaraya: Engineer & Nation-Builder*, Rupa & Co, New Delhi.

Salwi, Dilip M., *S. Chandrasekhar: The Scholar Scientist*, Rupa & Co, New Delhi.

Salwi, Dilip M., *S.N. Bose: The Immortal Scientist*, Rupa & Co, New Delhi.

Santapank, H. (Ed), *J. Sen Memorial Volume*, J. Sen Memorial Comm. & Botan. Soc of Bengal, Kolkata.

Sharma, O.P., *Great Men of India*, Uppal, New Delhi.

Shirazi, P.P.P., *Sixteenth Century Indian Scientists*, Hindustan Publications Corp, Delhi.

Singh, Jagjit, *Some Eminent Indian Scientists*, Publications Div, New Delhi.

Sitaramiah V., *M. Visvesvaraya*, Publications Div, New Delhi.

Venkataraman, G., *Journey into Light: Life and Science of C.V. Raman*, Penguin, New Delhi.

Vidya, G.M., *Jagadish Chandra Bose*, Vidharbha Marathwada, Pune.

Visvesvaraya, M., *Memoirs of My Working Life*, National Book Trust, New Delhi.